THE OPPOSITE OF LOVE

The
OPPOSITE
of LOVE

EMPOWERS WOMEN

KNOW THE NARCISSIST'S MIND, PROTECT YOUR HEART,
KNOW HOW TO SLAY THE DRAGON,
FOR THE LIFE YOU DESERVE

VICKI MILLS, MS, M.Ed.

The Opposite of Love
Empowers Women: Know the Narcissist's Mind, Protect Your Heart
Know How to Slay the Dragon, for the Life You Deserve

ISBN: 9798335577694

Editors: Mary Todd, Danna Mathias Steele
Cover Design, Vicki Mills, Danna Mathias Steele
1ˢᵗ Edition, 2024
Printed in the United States of America

To all women survivors; healing, thriving and living their best lives.
You are strong, beautiful, brave and resilient!

To my family and the precious women in it, for your generosity, wisdom, beauty and strength. My mother Violet always with me in spirit, mother-in-law Pamela; daughters Jennifer and Lynne who help so many; granddaughters Jillian, Violet and little great-granddaughter-on-the-way, Jaylene; who are and will make the world better with their extraordinary gifts and goodness. May your futures be filled with love, joy, purpose, and safety; in a world without discrimination.

Thank you for inspiring me every day.

TABLE OF CONTENTS

"Don't let the behavior of others destroy your inner peace." Dalai Lama

Introduction

This book is for anyone who wants to know how to avoid the pain of narcissistic relationships, deal with a person with narcissistic tendencies, stop the abuse, and take back their life from the dragon's jaws.

It is said that your wedding day should be one of the happiest days of your life. If that is true then the opposite can be said for the day you find out the man you married, the one you gave your heart to, is not the person you thought he was. I am writing this book for all women who either want to avoid, survive, or get over the pain of having had a committed relationship with a person who is only capable of self-love.

This Book Empowers Women

If you or anyone you know has been or are being hurt in a relationship, marriage, or divorce with a narcissist, this book will give you the "must-have" knowledge to break the cycle of manipulation, control, and abuse. Once you are able to spot red flags, you will have the ability to stay out of abusive relationships. If you are already emotionally involved with a narcissist, you have given some of your own power to him. You will learn how to regain your sense of self-worth and reconnect with your inner strengths, by using the knowledge and tools in this book. The beauty of knowing your own power is to understand you always have choices. Many times, we fall victim to believing we are powerless without choices. That's what the narcissist wants you to believe.

I have spent most of my life dealing with difficult people. As a life-long educator I am turning my years of lived experiences, the "how's" and "why's" of people's behavior who exhibit a high number of narcissistic characteristics into know-how to better deal with difficult situations. These understandings and skills are designed to help you maintain balance, your sense-of-self, come out stronger, and wiser with much needed confidence.

Every chapter highlights different areas to bring understanding to the subject of narcissism. Taken as a whole, it should give you a comprehensive blueprint to make the best of bad experiences. In education, we talk about teachable moments. I feel like my whole life has been filled with teachable moments. Now I am able to look back and pass on to you, hard-won lessons along with hundreds of hours of research. I am adding personal experiences to help you see how easily you can be tricked into believing things that are not true. The stories are meant to enhance your understanding of the way narcissists use many different tactics for control to give you power, when you may feel powerless.

Relating to these stories will raise your awareness allowing you to see through the smoke screens, hear the intentions behind the words, and know how to better deal with the narcissist in your life. Once you are knowledgeable about different aspects of narcissism, your consciousness will be raised and you will not be taken in by toxic people.

If you are already in an abusive relationship, you will learn how to flip the script to protect yourself from further harm. Remember, you give your power away, when you allow another person to abuse you. You lose yourself when you stay with that person. You will learn how to take your power back. The power imbalance is what makes you miserable.

You will learn how childhood abuse may have predisposed you to stay in a narcissistic relationship. The best safe-guard against narcissistic abuse is to have a good sense-of-self, and the confidence to not put up with it. The narcissist is very cunning and can be immensely charming. Your armor against his charm will be the knowledge of what he is actually doing.

My intension for writing this book is for you to have the insight that will help you avoid falling into a narcissist's trap, deal with him in a healthy way, break the cycle of abuse and ultimately live the life you deserve.

Why I Have Written this Book for Women

Statistically, we know there are more diagnosed male narcissists than female ones. We also know women are disproportionally abused by their male partners. That puts the bulk of the painful lifelong, debilitating trauma on women.

Of course, even though it was written from a woman's point of view, with women in mind, I want to welcome anyone to read it for its value to you. I am sure you can find useful information in this book. It was said to me that, this book is a "meal" which serves up the kind of relationship knowledge people are hungry for. I have spoken to people with narcissistic boyfriends, spouses, bosses, doctors, and relatives, who would benefit from the information presented here. This tremendous amount of pain needs to be replaced with understanding, healing and love.

Questions We Will Be Answering

- What are the most important things you need to know about narcissism?
- How can you spot a narcissist, early?
- How can you find out if a prospective partner or current husband/partner is a narcissist?
- Does the label matter?
- How did they become a narcissist?
- Why are you attracted to these types of men?

- How do you get hooked by them?
- Why were you chosen for this role of a narcissist's partner?
- Is it ever your fault?
- Why do you stay in toxic relationships?
- How do you deal with the lying, cheating, and betrayal?
- What can you say to a narcissist to gain your power back?
- How to tell a covert narcissist from an overt and why is it important to know the difference?
- What should you watch for and do when he shows you his true self?
- Why is it so dangerous to stay in a narcissistic relationship?
- How do you move on, gain back your confidence, and take back your life?

The "Dragon" Side of a Narcissist's Personality

You will gain insight to when and how to say no, set boundaries, and navigate the murky waters of the narcissist's personality. It will be hard to believe, but there really is a dragon beneath all that charm, ready to spit fire at the first sign of a perceived threat or if told no. You never want to be on the receiving end of that!

I believe the meaning of the title of this book is the key to unlocking the secrets inside the narcissist's mind. Knowing how a narcissist thinks will protect you from being blindsided by his behavior. Most people have no idea that narcissists create false identities, which they live behind. This way of living is just too foreign. When the dragon side of the narcissist's personality comes out, there is so much more to what you are witnessing. It is not just anger. You will find out where it comes from, how to deal with it and what it really means. Knowing his distorted view of the world and how opposite it is from your own reality, will give you the power to not fall back into another narcissistic relationship.

There is Good News!

Even though narcissistic behavior can be complex and puzzling, there is good news! There are predictable patterns of narcissist's behavior. Knowing these patterns, will enable you to see the trees, even in the thickest forest. The coping strategies, insights, and suggestions can guide you through abusive relationships and calm the chaos. While narcissistic relationships are definitely complex moving targets, with each person bringing their own unique experiences, there is light at the end of the tunnel!

A DIFFERENT POINT OF VIEW

I am not a clinician, but have plenty of experience with narcissists. In fact, I consider myself a serial narcissist's partner. This is not a badge of honor, but in my defense, this started way back in my life when I was too young to understand. Also, that was a different time in the world where the word narcissist was not thrown around like confetti as it is today.

Even now, with all this attention to this subject, instead of clarity, more questions are constantly surfacing. I felt compelled to add my voice, to share what I have learned because I think I have a different point of view. I have been personally devastated and found myself between homes. During one particular trying time, I moved across the country, because I knew that would be the only way not to be sucked back into a cycle of abuse. During that time, I remember saying to myself; *"Now I know how it happens when a person finds themselves living under a bridge"*. At that point, I was so devastated I had stopped eating and was beginning to scare myself because I seemed to be losing my will to live. Thinking you are drowning is a powerful motivator for change.

Coming back from the brink brings a fresh perspective. I had always been a supremely positive and optimistic person and had never been that low. I knew I had to do something fast. And so, I began to make plans to get my life back on track. The insights I am sharing with you here, were born out of heartbreak, deep reflection, and soul searching. I had to do the research and educate myself for my own stability and sanity. I had to call upon unknown inner strength to pick myself back up, do the work, and use my new-found knowledge to find freedom from the grip of past abusive experiences. That is why I am confident you can do it, too!

I have found it to be true that real learning comes from adversity, not from stress-free times. Just like building muscle; you must work them, even break them down, to build them back. Our emotional growth is also like that. When we are faced with difficult situations and overcome them, rising to meet occasions, is when real growth and progress is made. As the saying goes, "*There's more room in a broken heart*". Can't tell you how many times I told myself that.

This book is written to shine the spotlight on this subject, in a way that it is tailored to your needs. I am hopeful by adding my personal experiences with narcissistic personalities, you will see you are not alone. It is designed for you to apply what you will learn to your own situations.

In order to maintain power in their relationships, narcissists feel compelled to use various manipulation tactics to control you. Their goal is to keep you confused and off balance. This cloud of confusion will dissolve once you understand your situation.

Exploring Abusive Relationships

You will explore abusive relationships from the practical perspective of, "What do I do when I realize I am in one?", "How do I deal with a narcissistic partner?" Although it is important to understand certain terms, this book is leaving the clinical perspective to the clinicians.

You will see how different biochemicals made in your own body, influence your reactions in various emotional situations. This will help you understand some of the underlying reasons you act the way you do, as you are experiencing feelings of falling in love, and even unreasonable feelings of wanting to stay in an abusive situation. You will know how your body's own chemistry makes you become addicted to the feelings of being "in-love" and makes you vulnerable to the narcissist.

Being able to spot "love bombing", as a narcissistic tactic will keep your head and heart from being captured in a controlling relationship. If this book prevents pain and enables just one woman to break this cycle of control and abuse, then it has done its job!

Always remember, there is no substitute for professional help from an expert in this field. If you are being mentally or physically abused, please consult a licensed clinical psychologist. Physical abuse should never be tolerated! Community hotlines and safe houses are available to help women stay safe. In the United States, the National Domestic Violence Hotline is: 1-800-799-7233. It is staffed 24/7 and is available in 200+ languages. You can also reach them by text using the word; BEGIN TO 88788.

To thank you for buying this book, there is a companion website: www.theoppositeoflove.com The website will be available as a resource and where you can sign up to receive free information. I plan to post new research and insights, as they become available to support you. You will also find, "Bonus Chapters", tips, chat group answers and other helpful materials there. I will appreciate and look forward to any feedback from you that will help shed light on this subject. Please send your feedback and any questions through the website. Your feedback can further others' understanding of this subject.

Reviews are always appreciated because they let people know about this new way of looking at solving the problem of pain and abuse in narcissistic relationships. There is always more to learn!

"The opposite of love is not hate, it's indifference." Elie Wiesel

CHAPTER ONE

The Opposite of Love

Knowing the true meaning of the "Opposite of Love", will give you insight into the mind of the narcissist. Once you are aware of the true meaning of this phrase you will have a key to help you understand your narcissist's heart, or lack of it.

When asked the question, "What is the opposite of love?" most people would say "hate", but it is not hate, it is indifference. The understanding and application of the phrase, the opposite of love, came to me like a bolt of lightning, as an "aha!" experience. The realization of what is *not love*, but its opposite, gave me clarity about the chaos, the hurtful and confusing things which happened in various relationships. I am hopeful it will do the same for you.

One of the hardest things in a person's life is to find out the person they have pledged to spend the rest of their life with has betrayed their oath. You will gain precious insight into how the narcissist thinks once you are able to wrap your head around the concept of the absence of feeling for others, no empathy.

For the narcissist, this aspect of indifference takes away his responsibility for any wrong doing. He is always right when he is doing everything according to his self-serving rules. If he is indifferent to you, to your feelings, it allows him to continue to give 100% of his effort to satisfying his own needs, and justify everything he does.

A narcissist will never love you the way you want and need to be loved. He is incapable of digging deep into his emotions. That soul-connection you are seeking is not possible with a person with narcissistic personality disorder (NPD). They are too broken inside, too guarded to open their hearts to others. Whatever secrets and or insecurities they are hiding deep down prohibit them from completely opening up to you. Because they live in fear of rejection and shame, they cannot handle true intimacy.

A narcissist is good at fooling you into believing he loves you, but it will not be the true love you are seeking. He expends so much energy keeping up his false façade, he is incapable of real feelings for his partner. With this understanding, you can begin to see what you thought was love, is the opposite, and is in fact indifference. He convincingly plays the role of a person who cares.

It feels so real when he tells you he loves you. He doesn't just tell you; he may go overboard to show you. In the narcissist's world things are heightened and some things may feel a bit bombastic. Oversized gifts, or heaps of attention paid to you, things that might make you say to yourself, *"I never felt so loved"*. Is it possible that he means it in the moment? Yes, he means it, he can even feel it momentarily, but it is not the same "I love you" you are thinking of.

I LOVE YOU TO A NARCISSIST MEANS:
> *"I love you for what you can do for me"*,
> *"I love you for the way you make me feel"*,
> *"I love you for making me look good when we walk into the party"*.

Those are just a few examples. I am sure you might be able to fill in the blanks with some of your own.

A Prisoner of His Past

Our past has shaped us into who we are and the narcissist is no different in that respect. In fact, the narcissist is more a prisoner of his past experiences because something in his past stopped his emotional growth. He did not fully grow into emotional maturity. He is more sensitive to past hurts than most people. Where a healthy person can dig deep within themselves to find the strength to overcome whatever traumas they experienced, the narcissist cannot do that having shut down emotionally years before. The narcissist acts and reacts from how he views his world through that immature lens. His past pain keeps him in protection mode to stop from being put into painful situations again. Everything he does for you is conditional with implied reciprocations. This may not necessarily be "top of mind" for him, but in his world, relationships are always transactional. *If I do "x", I expect you to do "y".*

Why You Cannot Trust a Narcissist

If he is a smart narcissist, the covert ones usually are, he might be playing a complicated game with you. A game with many twists and turns, taking you through imaginary mazes with many dead ends.

These games are intended for securing his most complicated needs, so his games are calculated, complex, and hidden. One example: as he is "pulling the wool" over your eyes, he might at the same time be further manipulating you for another reason. He might be trying to get more admiration from you, by having you acknowledge how clever he is. For those of us who are unable to interpret "narcissist", and do not think that way, it is unfamiliar territory. For a loving, trusting partner, he might just as well be speaking a foreign language! Our minds just don't work that way.

The key words are love and trust. If you love someone you trust them. There is no real relationship, if there is no trust. How do you trust someone who thinks you are a fool for trusting them? But you do trust, as you are blind to his view of trust being a weakness to be used for control. Then one day, you wake up to the reality that he didn't deserve your trust in the first place.

MARY'S STORY: THE CLEVER COVERT
NARCISSIST MAKES FUN OF HER TRUST

Mary was married to a very clever covert narcissist. He was so clever that he was able to love bomb her into trusting him completely and to string her along for years. She was completely devoted to him. Every morning when she woke up, she felt like pinching herself to make sure she wasn't dreaming. She thought he was the perfect man; kind, good and always surprising her with gifts. He even insisted on doing all the cooking, which is something she loved about him.

In reality, Mary's husband George looked at her as not very smart, because she trusted him with everything in their lives. She even gave him her paycheck and he gave her an allowance. One day, he became impatient with her for not seeing his ability to keep her in the dark. He was doing so many things behind her back and became frustrated that it was too easy to fool her. Her devotion was not enough to satisfy him, anymore. He also wanted acknowledgement for how skillful he was in his deception. So, that day he started to move his hands, like a magician in front of her face. He kept moving his hands, each hand circling in a different direction. While doing that he said, "watch the hands, the left doesn't know what the right hand is doing". Of course, she wondered what he was doing, but being a non-confrontational person, she just smiled and shrugged it off. Not in her wildest dreams could she have imagined he had been cheating on her for the past year or more.

Many narcissists get energy from seeing their negative effect on others. A narcissist can mistake your caring and trust for stupidity because he is not capable of loving someone with all his heart. It is easy for him to look down on his partner, when he is convinced, he is the smarter one.

How Indifference Affects His Partner

Because of this absence of feeling, this indifference, we know truly out-rageous and hurtful things have happened to women (and of course to men, too). He can pronounce the relationship or marriage over when he finds his next new shiny object, leave home and possibly never come back. He may be so cruel as to flaunt the new affair. All that, without feeling guilt or remorse. He has that ability to justify whatever bad be-havior he does because of how he perceives himself in a relationship.

Because in his mind the relationship is conditional, if his wife stops giving him exactly what he feels he needs, wants, and deserves, he thinks whatever he does is OK. He is indifferent to anyone else's feelings. Once you understand this, you will see the relationship was not what you thought it was.

Your narcissist can turn into a raging dragon over the smallest thing. A narcissist's indifference to others' feelings affords him the luxury of acting out his anger whenever and wherever he wants. Impatience, petulance, silent treatment and sulking all are forms of anger that we might not see as abuse, but they are.

I am using the dragon image, spitting fire to represent how irate he can become. People have said, the narcissist is a vampire who sucks your life's blood. They blame narcissists for leaving you with little en-ergy or the will to live for yourself. I like the dragon metaphor better because it encompasses more of the narcissist's character traits and be-havior. My experience has shown me how the dragon's wrath allows him to intimidate, manipulate, and control his partner. The manipulation comes when his partner does his bidding without question, just to try to preempt or stop the rages. History has shown us, appeasing tyrants does not work, only setting boundaries and putting up "heat-shields" does.

JANE'S STORY: DRAGONS ARE TYRANTS

Jane tried to do everything to her husband's liking. She not only wanted to be "the perfect wife", she was basically programed to be one, from childhood. The problem was she was trying to balance it all. She worked hard all day, picked up the kids from two different schools, then once a week, the three of them would go food shopping.

One week, she was unable to find the particular brand of one of her husband's favorite snacks. He ate so much of this snack food, that he required her to buy more every time she went to the food store. Not only was she rushing around trying to get home in time to make dinner, but the kids were tired and cranky making her rush even more to get them home.

Finally, home Jane was putting away the groceries, when her husband came into the kitchen to inspect what she had bought. Not finding his favorite snack, but another brand of the same snack, he let his inner dragon out.

All of a sudden, Alex is slamming the kitchen cabinet doors, terrifying everyone while yelling about why he couldn't eat the snacks she had bought. Jane told him, in the calmest voice she could summon, she was not able to find his favorite brand. He was so upset, she stopped putting away the groceries. Even as tired as she was, knowing she still had the whole night ahead of her making dinner, washing up, throwing in a few loads of wash, getting the kids to bed; without a word, she was out the door on her way to another food store.

Dragons are tyrants and have you doing things you would not do for anyone else. Your narcissistic dragon can upset the harmony of your home with intimidation. If you feel you are walking on "eggshells" with your partner/husband, you are probably doing too much for him and not asking him to do enough. Remember, one-sided relationships don't work. They only cause stress for the person who is doing all the giving.

The reason for his outbursts may not be anything apparent, not even to him, but there is something there he does not want the world to see. That is why I talk about "slaying the dragon" in your relationship, because inside even the meekest and mildest narcissist, if poked, the dragon will appear!

The more you are aware of what he is doing and why he is doing it, the better you can neutralize his ability to manipulate and control you. Setting boundaries is a big part of keeping control of situations for your own safety. This is the beginning of you taking control and building a toolbox filled with your own tactics to getting your life back.

Narcissists Want to Keep Control

Another pitfall of being treated with indifference is he may attempt to keep his partner handy for further use even after boundaries have been established or the relationship has ended. Because of his indifference toward his partner, he has no problem stringing her along. Most people are uncomfortable with keeping their exes around so they do not string them along, but because of narcissistic indifference, they see no problem. There will be no thought of her needs If he thinks he can get more out of her, it is logical to him to keep her around.

MARY'S STORY: WILL YOU STILL BE MY BUSINESS PARTNER?

After Mary accidentally found out about her husband's cheating and living a double life, she still loved him and couldn't imagine a life without him. She gave him three months to give up his mistress. During those three months, he seemed to vacillate between wanting his mistress, then her, and some days he wanted them both. She knew she couldn't stay in that situation. She also knew how unhealthy and possibly dangerous it might be for her. He never let his inner dragon out but, indicative of the covert narcissist, when she was not cooperating with him, he quietly said, "I know some people". That was enough for her to hear, she knew from past conversations what he meant by that. She perceived it as a viable threat.

One day, when she was sure she was leaving, she asked if he would give her back her half of a down-payment they had put on an investment property. He acted surprised and said to her; "Oh, I thought you might want to keep that investment with me". Even after all that, he was still thinking of her supplying him with half the money needed to buy that investment and assuming she would want to stay in that business arrangement.

Smart Narcissists Think Steps Ahead

Narcissists can be super competitive. In his mind he must always win to validate his superiority. He must continually win because the walls he has built must never be breached. He has been living that life of calculating every situation for many years so he is very good at it.

This extreme love and protection of himself is shown in the need for constant acknowledgement, affirmation, admiration and absolute loyalty from his significant other and all those around him. It can become all-consuming for his partner who is trying to make him happy and making sure she doesn't have to deal with the dragon. He ensures his constant "supply" of this admiration from her, by using many different controlling tactics. His need for this supply can become more intense as time goes on. His partner might become like a drug dealer, where he is needing a stronger and stronger fix. Because he is addicted to getting his way, he will find new ways of getting them met. Many women have described this supply aspect of a narcissistic relationship as insatiable.

Whatever rules he sets may continue to change as he keeps moving the goal posts. For example: If he tells her she needs to lose 10 pounds to be more attractive, and she loses the weight, he might then say; *"I'd like you to change your hair-style"*. It doesn't matter to her narcissistic partner if his demands make sense to her, his indifference allows him to make demands without regard to what harm those demands may do. His indifference makes him oblivious to the effects of his actions on others.

Why Being Indifferent Can Make Narcissists Dangerous

Elie Wiesel was a Romanian-born American writer, Nobel Laureate, professor and Holocaust survivor. He wrote his memoir, "Night" to share with the world his experiences as a teenager in the Auschwitz and Buchenwald concentration camps, during World War II. His life's work was to speak out about human rights abuses. He said apathy and indifference is a greater threat to our way of life than hatred. He was one of the greatest advocates for peace and his work is powerful and lives on.

Hate is easy for people to understand. It is part of the human sphere of emotions. The word hate is even used by little children, as in: "I hate spinach". Feelings of hate for something, or someone can change over time. Indifference, on the other hand is not commonly talked about as an emotion. You hear people say, "Follow your passion", not "You need to give a damn". Indifference is usually associated with disorders and mental illnesses.

Indifference is foreign to us, hard to wrap our heads around, no feeling at all! With indifference, it is not fixable, it is not normal. It is the absence of feeling which can lead to disregard for other people's suffering and can turn into acts of extreme violence and inhumane cruelty.

Indifference is much more damaging to our psyches, you might say to our souls, because it truly is the opposite of what we have thought or felt is love. But, for the partner of a narcissist, indifference is confusing, leaving her to wonder what happened to that deep connection she was so convinced they had.

Healthy people do not deal well with indifference, they feel lost. Indifference leaves its target feeling less-than, not seen or heard, questioning their very existence. It can lead to profound loneliness and many times to depression. It not only robs her of her sense- of-self and self-esteem, but can shatter her life or even cause her to lose it. It is nothing to be taken lightly.

Knowing how a narcissist's indifference affects you can empower you to move forward. You will be able to see through the "smoke screen" by knowing the source of their arrogance and feelings of entitlement. Knowing you are not alone in suffering abuse in narcissistic relationships will validate your feelings and emotions. It can serve to lift your spirits and start you on a path of self-discovery and recovery.

TAKEAWAYS

- The opposite of love is indifference, not hate.
- Narcissists are indifferent to their partner's feelings, wants and needs because they are only dedicated to self-care.
- Narcissists are not capable of empathy.
- No empathy means they don't have the capacity to love in the way you want and need to be loved.
- Narcissists are able to convincingly playing the role of someone who cares.
- Indifference by a partner saps a person's strength and weakens their self-confidence. In its worst form, it can make them feel like a non-person and be soul crushing.
- The narcissist's dragon will erupt when there is a perceived threat to their thinly veiled façade of superiority and perfection.
- The acts of rage the dragon represents is how the narcissist shows his indifference to his partner. He gives himself permission to act out.
- The best way to deal with a narcissistic dragon is to stand up to him by setting boundaries for what behaviors you will not tolerate.

"Nothing can dim the light which shines from within." Maya Angelou

CHAPTER TWO

If I Knew Then, What I Know Now!

Your Inner Light

This quote by Maya Angelou is worth its weight in gold. It is your "Super Power". Being aware of your power and self-worth means you know you have the strength to not allow yourself to be subjugated by anyone. But this light can grow dim when you have given up power to another person. It will become more difficult to call upon, the more you push down the hurt and resentment from an abusive relationship. This is where you experience damage on the inside, when you don't stand up for yourself.

That inner light is your spirit, your deep reservoir of strength that we all have. Many people do not realize it is there and even more do not realize they can call it up when they need that strength. It is through adversity, when we are compelled to reach deep to find the right path, that we are able to appreciate the power of our own light.

Miraculously, the more you use that inner power, the stronger it grows and the more secure you feel in your strength. This limitless strength comes from love, the strongest force in the world. It is nourished and grows the more it is used. As you use your power to stand up for yourself, you are doing the opposite of allowing someone to abuse you.

Those of us who have had to pull ourselves out of the holes that we've allowed narcissists to put us in, come out stronger because we have discovered our truly resilient spirit. To reach down and find that inner power takes understanding that ending bad situations are opportunities to begin again, to do things a different way, to use our power for good, to love ourselves again and reset our lives for the better.

A narcissist, in their need to win, dominate, and control, will treat you in ways that dim your inner light. A partner who is not supportive, who tears you down, gaslights you into believing you are the problem, can make you feel less in touch with who you are. Over time, dealing with negativity, undermining, and disrespect weakens your ability to find your light. It also eats away at your self-respect as you work harder and harder to right a sinking ship. To stay in an abusive relationship takes a toll on your self-esteem. Some people living with abuse may turn to addictions in order to become numb to their situation. People who struggle with weight issues for example, are said to be "pushing down the hurt" literally with food. Some studies have shown that sugar is as addictive as cocaine, which means it messes with chemicals in your brain.

Addictions, as distractions, can give you temporary relief, but nothing can take away the pain. That makes it even more urgent and important to deal with the situation you are in, to find real, viable, and positive permanent solutions.

The longer the situation goes on, if you willingly give your power away, the harder it will become to stop. It is imperative for you to know you have the ability to reach deep, find your inner light, and take back your power!

Don't Lose Touch with Your Own Needs

Don't wait until others are asking you what's wrong, question yourself and listen to what you need to be secure in yourself. Listen to what your heart and mind are telling you.

JANE'S STORY: TWO QUESTIONS THAT CHANGED HER LIFE:

Jane said, "The best gift I received toward the end of a long marriage, was from a friend who genuinely wanted to know how I was. They asked because they knew I was feeling miserable and had been struggling for years."

*"**How are you feeling today?**" This is a question a narcissistic partner will never ask you, they don't want to hear the answer, unless they think it might score points, or they can use your answer against you.*

*"**What do you really want?**" That question was a game-changer for Jane, because it was the one question she had been afraid to ask herself. She said, "I knew there was no good answer. Just a lot of bad choices." "At that point, I had lost so much of my sense of who I was in that marriage, it felt like I didn't even know what I wanted. All I knew for sure was I wanted to end the pain of feeling totally lost, disrespected, and not seen or heard."*

Many times, when we are in bad situations, our "go-to" thinking may be that we don't have choices. Then the narcissist partner has us right where he wants us, "stuck". But, if we don't make choices for ourselves, we have no one to blame but ourselves.

JANE'S STORY: DISRESPECT CAN HURT A WHOLE FAMILY

Ten years before Jane finally realized how hopeless her marriage was, an incident happened to show her that her husband didn't respect her.

She knew their parenting styles were totally different, but was blind-sided when he decided to step in as she was disciplining one of their children. This particular afternoon,

*he was home and overheard them talking. Her way was
to talk over with the child what they had done and come
to a punishment that they both agreed on. Her husband,
without warning ran over to the child, picked her up, put
her in her room, and then shoved Jane into their bedroom.*

At that moment, Jane was reduced to a non-person. This was a total undermining of her authority as a parent. Jane didn't realize what was at stake. How the husband treats his wife sets an example for their children. Why hadn't she fought back and not let him treat her this way? She foolishly traded her dignity and authority for what she thought would bring peace to their home. It had the opposite effect. It turned out to be too high a price for her to pay.

Appeasement doesn't work with a narcissist. They just get stronger the more you give in to them. You are feeding the dragon. Sadly, this show of lack of respect can make a powerful impression on a child and make the child disrespect you, as well. It is a very bad precedent to set and undermines the whole family dynamic. This also makes gaining back respect difficult to impossible, when you allow your spouse to take away your parental authority.

This narcissistic tactic of treating his partner like a child or demeaning her career as not being as important as his, is used for his control, while elevating the narcissist's position in the family. If you don't have the tools to know how to handle those controlling actions, or even realize you are in an abusive situation, it is tough to do anything meaningful to stop that abuse and the damage it causes.

She was not proud of where she was in that marriage, but because she had put so much of her energy into trying to feed the dragon, she had basically given up on trying to gain back the respect that would have automatically been there if she had married a supportive husband. The biggest problem was she didn't want to recognize she had a problem. They had been together for so long, that his actions had become normal events. She did not have the tools to know what to do about his behavior, or the maturity to know they were hurting the whole family. Ignoring problems does not make them go away.

Don't sweep things under the rug, leaving unanswered questions. If something doesn't feel right, keep questioning until you get an answer that makes sense. If your partner tries to avoid answering, or gets upset with you for asking, then you have a good idea something is not right. This will give you a better idea of what you are dealing with. If there is nothing wrong, then it should be easy for him to give a plausible answer.

MARY'S STORY: THE VINTAGE DRESS

> *One beautiful evening, they got dressed up and went downtown to attend an opera. George had season tickets. Mary decided to wear a dress she had saved for a special occasion just like this. It was from another era. It was all black with lace and sequin accents, it exuded "Old Hollywood Glam". She topped it off with some very pretty jewelry and felt on top of the world. George looked very handsome in a lovely new suit with his favorite cuff-links. As they approached the magnificent theater, she could see couples were being stopped to have their photos taken. She wasn't sure what was going on, but she was hoping they might get stopped. It would be a real first for her! To her surprise, that dress caught a producer's eye and they were singled out to have their photo taken. Mary couldn't wait for the next month's issue to come out. She wanted so much to see them in there as a couple.*

> *The next month, as she read the new issue of the "Who's Who at the Opera", she was disappointed not seeing their photo in the magazine. The next day, she checked with the magazine and was told, "The photo did not go into the magazine because someone said they thought she was his mistress and it would be embarrassing for him". She*

laughed at the thought, his mistress, how crazy? She took
it as a compliment. It never crossed her mind, that this
person, who was trying not to embarrass her husband,
might have known something she didn't.

When a Narcissist Lies and When He Tells the Truth

If you catch him in a lie, you must not believe him. Don't make excuses for him. You can be quick to make up reasons to believe him. If he lies to you, he is a liar. Don't accept his lies at face value and be aware he will continue to do it, especially the more he sees he can get away with it.

When he tells the truth, believe him. He is often not believed. You will want to believe him because he may be revealing what he is actually doing and who he is. If you can see through the mist of being "in love," long enough to have it register, you will be able to gain important information about his true intensions.

One of the most common mistakes women make is they don't take to heart things men tell them if they don't want it to be true. One common example with many men, not just narcissists, is when a man says, "I don't want to have children". A woman hearing that and not wanting it to be true, can rationalize what she heard with a type of "magical-thinking". She might tell herself; "*Oh, he will change his mind, once we are married*", or "*He will change his mind, when he sees how good we are together and what good parents we will make*". This kind of thinking doesn't include him. It is dangerous because it is not dealing with reality which may come back to bite.

Narcissists Put Themselves First

A narcissist has very specific requirements in any relationship. His disorder puts demands on the relationship because his partner, in addition to the regular give and take in relationships, must be willing to put up with him getting his way and setting the rules. When first dating a narcissist may warn you about himself. Of course, when you are in the beginning of the relationship, you are thinking, "He is perfect, what is he talking about?"

When most people talk about "love language" they are talking about the ways people express and receive love. They may express affection by giving gifts or doing things for others. Other people may show love in physical touch or spending time together. Most people's love language includes wanting to make each other happy.

A narcissist's love language is not what you are imagining. He is not saying let's find out what makes each other happy and do this for each other. When a narcissist says, "I love you", he is saying I am ready for you to worship me and fulfill all my needs. You are not necessarily in the equation, other than to be there for him. That is why the narcissist's partner is sometimes referred to as "supply". That is a dehumanizing label, but it serves a very important and useful purpose to highlight the way a narcissist looks at his partner. Remember, it is the "Opposite of Love", whether consciously or subconsciously, he sees her for what she can do for him.

He only listens to one radio station, WIIFM. WIIFM, means what's in it for me! If you keep that in mind, once you're considering someone as a possible partner, or even if you are already in a narcissistic relationship, it will help to be more clear-eyed and realistic about your expectations. It is difficult to know for sure what narcissists are up to, outwardly charming, but tricky and secretive when playing their control games.

JANE'S STORY: THE IRATE MOTHER, SETTING BOUNDARIES

Many years ago, Jane was teaching in a private school. The children there were financially privileged, but emotionally deprived.

On a particular "Open House" day, a mother stopped Jane and wanted to talk. She was visibly upset about her son not getting the grade she felt he deserved. The mother

told Jane something she had only seen and heard in mov-
ies. Pointing her finger in Jane's face she said; "If you don't
change his grade, I will see to it that you never work in
this town again". Jane pulled herself up to her full height,
and said, "You cannot threaten me, I am used to being
threatened by a professional."

By professional, Jane was referring to the level of abuse she was getting at home from years of living with her husband Alex. Even though Jane was able to stand up to the "irate mother", she was still making excuses and tolerating the dragon at home. This shows how normalized her homelife had become. When faced with something similar, outside the home Jane was able to deal with it by sticking up for herself. But experiencing Alex's behavior at home, was a problem because she did not view his behavior as abuse. You cannot defend yourself or set boundaries, until you are able to see it as actual abuse.

It is not easy to stay a step ahead of the narcissist in your life. But you are not alone. So many people are going through this and there is a lot of caring help out there. For you to guard against falling under a narcissist's controlling tactics, such as gaslighting and smoke-screening, you must confront and question the lies, confront the put downs and do your best to not accept harmful behavior. To not confront and ultimately trust a narcissist is dangerous because he is very good at using these tactics to dominate, manipulate, and control his partner. If you accept his lies as truth, you hand over your power and could possibly be giving him full control of your life. Being too trusting, complacent, and non-confrontational could have consequences for the rest of your life!

On the other hand, if you know you have choices, you will have learned that the love you hold in your heart, the endless light you have within you is precious and needs to be cultivated, protected and never underestimated!

When you have an issue to face, stand up to it, don't think it will go away on its own. Know you always have choices to be able to get to the life you want. The choices may not be easy, but we only find out how strong we are when we dig deep, call upon our inner light and power. Using our inner light to guide us, will always bring us back to who we are. Use your light to light the way back to yourself and to help others.

TAKEAWAYS

- Don't lose touch with your own needs. Don't be afraid to call on your own inner strength when you need it.
- Ask yourself: How are you feeling today? What do you really want?
- Confront and question lies, find out the truth and never make excuses for a liar.
- Narcissists put themselves first, always.
- Your light is your strength and power that shines bright within you through love.

"Ignorance is not bliss, it's the darkness that keeps us from seeing the light." Unknown

CHAPTER THREE

Know How to Spot a Narcissist

This chapter is the map that can lead you on a journey out of an unknown place into a brighter future of empowerment. Just like traveling with GPS, the characteristics of narcissists are your prompts showing you where that road may lead. Knowing what to look for in a partner puts you on the road to having good decision-making skills, which will lead to making better choices This clearer vision is the beginning of building up your resistance to a narcissist's charm offensive. Being familiar with these "tell-tale" signs of narcissism, you will be able to determine if a prospective love interest's narcissistic characteristics are "deal breakers", and not try to excuse their behavior.

When faced with one of these individuals, you will be able to reach into your toolbox of knowledge for the insight to see what's happening and what you need to do. Having this clearer vision and skills could save you from years of heartache.

Spotting a Narcissist is the Number One Skill

You must be able to identify who he is before you can know how to deal with him. Because narcissists can be illusive, hiding behind their made-up personas, the art and science of "narc-spotting" is the way to keep control of your life. Once you are aware of what to look for, things will become much easier.

COVERT AND OVERT NARCISSISTS

There are two main types of narcissists. It is worth noting that "overts" and "coverts" express their characteristics differently. This shows up in different patterns of behavior.

The overt narcissists are easier to spot as they seem to take up more space in the room, being outwardly bold characters. The covert narcissist can be much more secretive and cunning, concealing their narcissistic characteristics, making it more difficult for their partner to discover who they truly are.

Watch for These Main Characteristics

These characteristics are the most important ones and seem to be the most agreed upon and universally accepted by the experts. They are a good starting place when trying to determine if your partner, or perspective partner might be a narcissist.

1. **No Empathy**
2. **Grandiose Sense of Self-Importance**
3. **Need for Excessive Admiration**
4. **Sense of Entitlement**
5. **Arrogance and Superiority**
6. **Exploitive Behavior**
7. **Preoccupation with Fantasies of Success and Power**
8. **Lack of Accountability**
9. **Fragile Self-Esteem**
10. **Play Fast and Loose with the Truth**

A Deeper Dive into How Narcissistic Characteristics Translate into Behavior

Unable to Show Empathy This is the number one trait of a narcissist The lack of ability to see when another person is hurting or in need of help, leaves them missing a large part of a healthy personality. They are so preoccupied with their own feelings they are void of caring. Much of this lack of empathy goes back to their incomplete emotional development.

These two narcissistic characteristics are linked: Lack of empathy and lack of self-awareness. A person who lacks self-awareness can say and do things that hurt others because they have no understanding of how their behavior affects others.

The Dalai Lama's teachings say: "The purpose of life is to seek happiness through love, empathy and positive actions." Without empathy a narcissist can only relate to others on a superficial level. You can never have a healthy relationship with a person who cannot appreciate your feelings.

Grandiose Sense of Self-Importance/ Competitiveness – *"Can you believe it? "George would say in a disgusted tone of voice".* His stress of the day showed on his face while he complained to Mary about how his whole department was going to go to "hell", because they had not used his brilliant suggestion. He seemed to need to put others down to lift himself up. Narcissists lack respect for others. It is easy for male narcissists to feel puffed up and bully anyone they feel are lower on the "pecking order". Society has already bestowed upon them a feeling of superiority over woman.

His constant quest for self-importance turns even the most mundane things into a competition. Their fragile ego demands it. That is why they ruin events, break up friendships, and down-play other people's experiences.

JANE'S STORY: "THE PAPASAN CHAIR"

> When Jane's daughter was a baby, she would sit her up in a large round "Papasan" chair, put on music, and dance for her. The baby seemed to really enjoy it, as her little body wiggled

in the chair moving to the music. Once, in the middle of this dancing, her husband Alex came into the living room and abruptly turned off the music, with no explanation.

Narcissists don't want to see others having fun, if they are not a part of it or didn't initiate it. They can be real "party poopers".

MY STORY: A MAGAZINE COVER PHOTO

I was so excited to show my mother a photo I had taken of an airplane which appeared on the cover of an aviation magazine in England. My husband was an aviation photographer and he had encouraged me to take photos of the planes when they appeared with a new color scheme. What made my photo interesting enough to be a cover photo was because it was the first time this color scheme appeared on a much larger plane, than the rest of the fleet. As I showed my mother the cover of the magazine and how I'd been credited with my photo, she said, "Does your husband know your photo is on the cover?" "If I were you, I wouldn't tell him."

She thought she was giving me good advice on how to shield him from the "horrible" knowledge that I had gotten a cover photo, when his photos had been on multiple magazines for many years. She just assumed all men had such fragile egos that they were intimidated by a woman's success.

I had the pleasure of telling her my husband was the one who sent my photo to the magazine. He was not threatened by me, in fact just the opposite. Not only had he taught me what I need to know to be an aviation photographer, but he was fostering my pursuit and took pleasure in my success. A man who can put his ego aside to support others, is not a narcissist.

Constant Need for Excessive Admiration – There are men who are lucky enough to be in wonderful relationships, but there are others who after losing one relationship have to move quickly into another one. They are afraid of living alone. Usually, healthy people can find it within themselves to take the time to process what they are going through without having to have another person in their life right away. Many narcissists already have their next victim picked out while they are still in their current relationship. These types of men need every form of adulation, appreciation, attention, approval, and validation. Some narcissists attach themselves to people who may look or act like what they want for themselves. In severe cases you might find people who will want to be someone else. They show this by idolizing the person so much, they start to look and act like them.

Sense of Entitlement – A narcissistic personality has been created by them over time to reinforce in themselves that they are great, that they deserve everything they want. Their fragile ego compels them to live up to that. Their sense of entitlement makes them look confident on the outside, when inside, they are scared little boys. They lead with this, to portray themselves as a person who expects special treatment. Their sense of entitlement supports their idea that they are superior to others and it is OK for them to act any way they want. They use it to excuse their harmful behavior as they are convinced their needs are more important than anyone else's and are able to ignore the harm they do.

MY STORY: THE ENTITLED DOCTOR TO THE DETRIMENT OF HIS PATIENT

After a robotic surgery, my doctor visited my room that afternoon and proudly showed me a photo of my insides that the computer had taken. But it was not my photo, it had another patient's name on it. He didn't apologize. In the late evening of that day, I started to feel uncomfortable, feeling very heavy. The nurses tried to tell me that was normal. By midnight, I had retained so much water I couldn't turn over in the bed. As luck would have it, right outside my room someone had left a scale. When I got on it, I couldn't believe my eyes. I had gained 17 pounds! I waddled to the nurses' station to tell them. Again, they tried to tell me it was normal to feel bloated because during that type of operation air is pumped inside you. I told them, air cannot possibly be an explanation for a weight gain of 17 pounds. I knew there was something very wrong going on with me. They refused to call the doctor saying, "We have strict orders not to call this doctor after midnight." "He will yell at us." As it turned out, when he arrived the next morning, my body chemistry was off from the operation and even he had to admit my situation was dire. He said he got there just in time, to order the meds to reverse my chemical imbalance. He had used his entitlement, as a doctor to intimidate the staff to the point that they ignored my situation and even he had to admit I was about to go into shock and it put me in danger.

Arrogance and Superiority – This feeling that they are better than others goes hand-in-hand with the last one, In their minds, the sense of entitlement, feelings of superiority and acting arrogant lessen the chance they will be challenged. Being challenged is a problem for them because of their need to protect what is really going on inside of them.

Many narcissists rely heavily on having a good appearance: well groomed, well dressed, take good care of themselves. None of these things are bad on their own, but when it comes to being one way to the outside world and another to the people close to you, then there is a problem. Narcissists seem to know the right things to say to a woman, they might come off a bit too smooth. This red flag warns they may have had a lot of practice in saying just the "right" things to manipulate women.

Many narcissists have good, high paying, prestigious jobs. Certain professions attract people with different personality disorders, because those professions coincide with their made-up image. They may have worked hard to gain their skills because they are so competitive, but not for completely healthy reasons. People look up to them, they command attention with their appearance and expertise. This statement is based on research done over many years about specific professions and personality disorders.

Exploitive Behavior – We all know what the word exploitation means, but how do narcissists take advantage of their partners? The examples of this are endless. The narcissist may choose a person for what she has to give. A narcissist may even tell her what attributes are attractive to him. A woman may think these are compliments, but he might be just listing things about her in order to fill out his wish-list. Whatever the partner has to give, the narcissist is a master at getting it and more. He can charm his partner into doing things she would not do for anyone else. He might have her do things under the guise of proving her love, loyalty, or anything that suits his fancy. He can be deceptive; finding out her dreams and falsely promising he will make them come true. He might lead a double life, have more than one woman. To him women are expendable.

He might want to control the money, her energy, or even her interactions with other people. Some narcissists might not have a lot of friends and want yours. Sometimes they might even want to be you. That may be why they have been dubbed "vampires", sucking the life out of their partner.

Preoccupation with Fantasies of Success and Power. – This is another one that correlates to their feelings of entitlement, arrogance and superiority. Many narcissists are successful people because they are driven to exceed, but no matter how much they have, they always fantasize about being even more successful and powerful.

Lack of Accountability – They cannot take responsibility for their actions, or how their actions affect others. They feel too vulnerable to let other people in, protecting themselves from being seen. This is why they deflect criticism and project blame onto others.

If you point out a nasty remark he made and try to tell him how it made you feel, his reaction might be to say some things like these gems;

"No, I didn't mean it that way",

"No, you are too sensitive and taking it the wrong way",

"No, I was only joking".

"No, I didn't say that!" (This is true gas-lighting to make his partner doubt her own hearing and memory.)

Fragile Self-Esteem – His self-esteem is fragile because he is hiding shame or weakness. His extreme protection of his fragile inner self can lead him to feel easily threatened. His reactions can be extreme, might even become paranoid about perceived slights. His fragile ego can also play a role in jealous behavior. If he's the best, then how can anyone else be better? If he feels slighted or questioned, the "dragon" side of his personality comes out to defend him.

Play fast and loose with the truth – Because a narcissist lives in his self-created unrealistic bubble, he is literally living a lie about who he is. This makes it almost impossible for him not to lie. The ones who are high on the narcissistic scale, may believe their own lies, which makes their false façade feel even more real to them. Not all people with narcissistic traits lie, but the ones who lie consistently, are not to be taken lightly, and might also be prone to doing harm to others. Some narcissists don't openly lie to their partners, but if she listens to what he says to others, especially when he is talking on the phone, she might see a different side of him. Getting support from a professional is a good way to help you deal with those kinds of situations.

The Meaning of the Dragon's Image on the Cover

You may think I am being dramatic when I say a narcissistic person can turn into a "fire-breathing" dragon. I am using the dragon as a metaphor for a narcissist's rage, their melt down. This can be very serious, having dangerous consequences for both the narcissist and his partner. Rage is anger that has gotten out of control to the point that the chemicals in his body are fueling his conduct. This anger is usually a manifestation of feelings of fright or shame.

For example: if he has convinced himself he is the smartest person in the room and something he says is questioned, he might lose his ability to control his anger. It doesn't matter if the threat to his self-concept is real, his go-to emotion is to lash out and make the other person pay for what he has perceived as a threat or slight.

Although he doesn't literally breathe fire, the actions of the dragon persona are a scary thing to experience. If you have ever experienced that, you will never doubt the need to protect yourself from it. As you might imagine, this is how women can become victims of physical abuse. And if liquor or drugs are involved that will be a toxic mix.

Just like the drawing on this book cover, where a seemingly happy couple is gazing into a mirror together, what they are seeing in their reflection is not what they were expecting. She sees him in a completely different way. Even though they are looking at an obviously fictional character, it represents what it is like to be the partner of a narcissist when he is triggered. A look behind the mirror, so to speak.

Comparison of a Healthy Relationship to Life with a Narcissist

In the beginning, your new love will exude charm and seem "oh-so" perfect. He will say and do all the right things. But there is a pattern to the way relationships progress, and if he turns out to be a narcissist, watch out for bumpy roads ahead! Life is always filled with twists and turns, and all relationships are tested by stress from events beyond their control. How you navigate together through the hard, uncertain times shows your commitment to each other and to the relationship. Narcissists are not fully developed emotionally, so they have a hard time dealing with any stress in their lives. Because of this they cannot support anyone else.

In healthy relationships, challenges you work through together should bring you closer. A commitment to make a life together is supposed to cement that relationship, as you go through life, putting your "loved-one's" needs above your own. You make compromises for the sake of that relationship and that's what makes it grow stronger. Narcissist's find it difficult to compromise.

7 KEY ELEMENTS OF HEALTHY RELATIONSHIPS VS. UNHEALTHY RELATIONSHIPS WITH A NARCISSIST PARTNER

1. **Honesty and Trust** are the bedrock of a healthy relationship, both partners feeling safe and secure because they have that trust in each other that each one's intensions are for the good of their relationship. The trust is what says to your partner no matter what, you can count on me to be there for you.
    -   In a relationship with a narcissist, trust is misplaced because their intensions are not always known and most of the time they are not for the benefit of their partner, because they are only true to themselves.

2. **Respect** is mutual, where both partners value the other's feelings, opinions and boundaries, treating each other with kindness, care and consideration.
    -   Respect is not present in a toxic relationship. Disrespect is used as a tactic for control by belittling to keep the upper hand in their relationship. This turns into self-doubt on her part which is damaging to her mental health.

3. **Boundaries** are a big part of a healthy relationship, where each partner understands the other's need for personal space, and autonomy, as they share their lives together. This doesn't happen without respect.
    -   Narcissists do not understand boundaries. In their world everything is all about them. This compels them

to blur lines between themselves and their partner. This leads to control and stomping on their partner's personhood. They are also capable of being jealous of something their partner has in an attempt to get that for themselves or being afraid of losing.

4. **Commitment** means when both partners want to do the work, doing whatever it takes to ensure a long-lasting and loving relationship.
   - In the relationship with a narcissist partner there is no permanent commitment to another person, because he can only love himself. If there is a commitment, it is conditional. When conditions change, so does his commitment.

5. **Unconditional Love** is given freely, without demands, or implied reciprocation in a healthy relationship. There is no pressure on either partner to earn the other's love.
   - In an unhealthy narcissistic relationship, there is no such thing as unconditional love. Narcissists are not able to give love freely. Love is always based on conditions.

6. **Support** is how each partner shows they empathize with their partner. Their concern for them is consistent, which gives their partner peace of mind, as they are there to mutually help each other achieve their goals and dreams.
   - Support is lacking with narcissists; in fact, it might be just the opposite. After convincing their partner they will be there forever for them, they may undermine their partner to further their own agenda.

7. **Communication** in healthy relationships, both partners feel comfortable expressing their thoughts without feeling judged. They acknowledge each other's concerns and if

there is a breakdown in communications, they are willing to work to make it better.

- Narcissists have many problems with communications. It is not straightforward; their partner cannot take them at their word and their passive-aggressive swipes are used to tear down his partner's sense of self to manipulate her. You cannot have good communication without trust, truthfulness, unconditional acceptance of the other person and a willingness to compromise.

FLEXIBILITY VS. RIGIDITY

People in relationships either grow together or they grow apart. In life nothing is static, nothing stays the same. In a one-sided relationship, there will come a time when it becomes impossible to stay together. It is not a relationship, when only one person is doing all the giving and it is not being reciprocated. Narcissists can carry on a seemingly good relationship until life throws the couple a curve. The narcissist doesn't have the emotional tools to deal with conflict or stress. When there is a problem, a narcissist is unable to step up, compromise or be responsible. A narcissist cannot allow anyone to question him. He must demand full allegiance to his point of view in order to prop up the illusion of superiority. It is important to know the basis of this point of view to understand his behavior. One of his main weaknesses is this brittle and unyielding point of view.

A quote about the bamboo's superior strength has been attributed to a Japanese proverb: *"The bamboo that bends is stronger than the mighty oak that resists"*. In other words, if you don't bend you will break. The more flexible you are, the stronger you will be. If you are flexible, you have the ability to change course in the face of adversity. I learned this from studying martial arts, and have heard many variations of it throughout Asia. The lesson of the bamboo's pliability symbolizes the way life's energy flows. Because life is dynamic, always changing; flexibility is a must for a good life and rigidity symbolizes death. We all need to be more like the bamboo in our lives. The narcissist's kryptonite is his inflexibility because of the ridged walls he lives behind.

What You Need to Do to Protect Yourself

Here are some meaningful and helpful ways to deal with a person who has narcissistic tendencies:

Educate yourself to be able to know who he is as quickly as possible. You're already doing this by reading this book. Having this knowledge helps you spot "Red Flags" and know not to ignore them. There are clinically recognized characteristics that go into defining a person who has NPD.

Know and understand the tactics they employ. If you know their game you can stop it before they are controlling and using you.

Know how to avoid getting drawn in by them. Understanding what you are dealing with and the purpose for those behaviors will help you build your own toolbox of strategies to use when needed.

Know yourself, your own strengths and weaknesses for dealing with and deflecting his tactics. Sometimes we are not in touch with ourselves and do not have the confidence we need to reach deep to find our strengths. But this is the way we grow, gaining confidence in our abilities as we move forward. The more difficult a situation, the more we learn about who we are.

Sometimes you may get lucky and things just work out for you, but so often flying blind in these types of situations turns out very badly for women. You need to know you already have everything you need within you. You can take charge of your life and live it the way you want to live it! By knowing yourself and understanding what they are doing, you will be able to "slay the dragon", ensuring a brighter and more healthy future for yourself.

Does it matter if He's a Certified Narcissist or a Person with Narcissistic Tendencies?

If you are getting hurt you are hurting, whether they have been diagnosed as being a person with a NPD or not. It might help to know if he is "certified" to be forewarned of the dangers of being in a relationship with a person like that. But, the probability of knowing that in advance will be slim to none, unless he is a public figure and books are being written about him. It is not a must or even possible to know where he falls on the narcissist spectrum for several reasons.

Only a small percentage of narcissists go to a professional who can diagnose their personality disorder(s). This is understandable knowing they are hiding who they really are. They have worked very hard to develop and maintain their façade of superiority, false as it may be. Most probably believe they do not need to be seen by a mental health professional. The most important things to know are what tactics they may use and how to deal with them when they are using them on you.

Character Traits that Stop a Narcissist from Seeking Help

- **He is defensive** – shuts down when he perceives a challenge.
- **He is in denial** – cannot admit to himself how broken and hurt he is.
- **His lack of self- awareness** - prevents him from being aware of his disorder.
- **He is unable to be vulnerable** – afraid to show his real self.

Narcissists' lives are ruled by the barriers they have put in place. It is a stressful way to live, when you are not living your truth. His barriers keep him on one side, emotionally cut off and everyone else on the other. This stops him from experiencing a full life. It also makes it difficult for him to seek help or confide in anyone. For people with NPD, needing help does not serve their concept of invincibility.

There are other reasons narcissists and people with other personality disorders do not seek help: They are not experiencing what their behavior is doing to the people around them, or they don't have the means or the availability of professional help in the area where they live.

Even the ones who admit they are narcissists may do so with pride, thinking it is a way of showing they are superior human beings, so they definitely don't feel a need for help. You may never know exactly what you are dealing with, or why he is the way he is, but that is not important if you know how to avoid or get out of a toxic relationship.

The most important ability for you is to be able to spot the narcissist and understand his game, so you can keep yourself from being harmed. The goal here is to make sure you do not become his victim and what to do if you are already in an abusive relationship. It is helpful to know how to deal with your narcissistic partner in ways that are healthy for you.

If the narcissist's mindset is to gain power over you, to satisfy whatever needs they have, then your weapon is knowledge. This gives you the advantage to decide a plan of action which is best for you. Mastering how to handle and negotiate through an abusive relationship and then surviving and thriving after you get out are this book's main reasons for being. So, hang on, there is a lot to learn.

TAKEAWAYS

- Learn the ten main characteristics of a narcissist.
- Each characteristic manifests into difficult behavior which can affect you when in a relationship with a narcissist.
- The appearance of "The Dragon" in a relationship is another type of control where he is using his rage as an intimidation tactic to make sure you are doing what he wants you to do.

- Knowing these characteristics and all that come with them will give you the knowledge to protect yourself.
- Even the mental health professionals agree, because of the complex nature of narcissistic personality disorder and the characteristic barriers in place, it is rare that a narcissist will seek help.
- What is needed to achieve a healthy relationship is missing in the narcissist's personality.

"You may not control all the events that happen to you, but you can decide not to be reduced by them." Maya Angelou

CHAPTER FOUR

Narcissists' Tactics

A person high on the spectrum of narcissism lies so much they actually believe their own lies. Narcissists control and manipulate people to keep their story going. They are only able to do that if you let them. You must willingly give your power to them. Their tactics are very powerful, but eventually most partners of narcissists begin to realize they are being hurt and start to push back against the narcissist's domination. They don't always recognize what the narcissist is doing and because they think they are in love with them, they will make excuses and apologies for their narcissist partner's behavior.

The narcissist themselves are not powerful, they know that deep down. That is why they fight so hard to conceal their truth selves, and employ all these different tactics. It is not a matter of if their partner will say they had enough, rather it is when the narcissist's bad behavior becomes too much.

No one falls for a narcissist knowingly. With an arsenal of control tactics, the narcissist can play on your emotions and even make you fall for him fast, before you actually get to know him. Once you fall, all the lovely promises may go out the window. He can use your goodness, trust, and empathy against you. Even sharing with him your wants, hopes, and dreams can become ammunition for his manipulation.

These tactics are mostly for control to ensure the narcissist gets his needs met. Some tactics are to degrade and keep their partner from knowing what they are up to. They maintain their false façade of superiority, to feed their feelings of self-worth. These tactics do just the opposite for the narcissist's partner, she loses her self-worth the more she allows herself to be manipulated by him.

The more you understand these tactics, the purposes they serve, and how they are used, the better you will be able to protect yourself. You will have the power to choose not to be abused because you know the game he is playing. The more you know, the more prepared you will be to control your own life or snatch it back from the dragon's jaws.

MAIN CONTROL TACTICS

Charm Offensive – This form of manipulation is what the narcissist uses in the early stages of their relationship. This is also sometimes called "love-bombing" or the "honeymoon" stage, which might be used over and over whenever he messes up and tries to woo his victim back with his charm. They win over their victims by being charismatic and confident, acting empathetic, interested, and attentive. They have a way of making a woman feel she is the only one in the room. When you are with a narcissist while he is wooing you, you will feel more "love" coming from him than you have ever felt. You need to remember, with them, everything is heightened because they are going after you and you are a great prize. They are super competitive and if they set their sights on you, they will go above and beyond to make that happen.

EMMA'S STORY: JERRY AND THE CHARMING HEART SHAPED BUD-VASE

> *Emma had been dating Jerry for about a year. They found they loved the same activities and were beginning to talk about taking their relationship to the next level. When*

Emma got a bad cold, Jerry was so charming, arriving at her door with chicken soup, a straw hat and a cane. Emma certainly understood why he brought the chicken soup, but why the straw hat and cane? To Emma's surprise and delight, he pulled out a small boom-box and began to dance for her wearing the straw hat, swinging the cane.

Jerry was always love bombing her with little gifts and thoughtful gestures. So, around Valentine's Day, after Jerry had talked about them sailing around the world together, he arrived with a beautiful bud vase in the shape of a heart containing one perfect rose.

That was Jerry, always thinking of her. But that day was different. He seemed distracted and said he had a lot to do and only stayed for a short time. Emma had begun to hear gossip about Jerry and other women.

With this in mind, Emma walked him to his car. She was looking for clues to his behavior. As she glanced at the back seat of his car she saw a large shopping bag. It contained three more identical charming bud vases, each with one rose. Not only was he deceiving her, but it turned out he had three more women "on the hook".

Twenty years later, she ran into Jerry and asked him how he could have done that. He told her he had found that if he asked women to sleep with him, every fourth one would. So, he did it because he could.

Emotional Manipulation – This tactic allows narcissists to get what they want from others. Some of the emotions that come into play are: guilt, shame, and fear. They are also very skilled at manufacturing stories to take advantage of their partner's empathy. Narcissists get their empath partner to pity them by telling stories of how they have been victimized, therefore tricking their partner into thinking they need help, when it is usually the other way around.

Isolation – A narcissist separates his victim from her support people, therefore creating a situation where she is relying on him more and more. She will be isolated from friends and family allowing him to gain more control over her emotions and her thinking. Within this realm, branding for isolation and controlling the narrative around their partner can be a very effective tactic. If a narcissist is able to brand their victim as a difficult person or an uncaring or selfish person, that "label" can stick. Think of the harm this does, as the recipient of this malicious branding not only loses loved ones, but continues to lose people in the future, as this myth about them is perpetuated. The more people the narcissist can turn against their partner, the more isolated they become and the more control he has.

Rage – A narcissist's anger stems from fear and shame. When a narcissist feels fearful or things are not going his way, he may lash out in a rage. It can be scary to witness and also because you do not know what kind of abuse is coming. He may just act moody or off kilter. Or he could be verbally and or physically abusive. A narcissist's rage, although discussed as a characteristic, becomes a tactic when used to intimidate his partner into fulfilling his wishes. If she is afraid of the "dragon" appearing, she will do things for him to make sure he doesn't show that side of his personality. She is being controlled just by the possibility of his rage appearing. The name for anticipating this "bad behavior", is preemptive obedience.

Over time, he may up his game when he wants to use rage for control. His partner who is trying hard to make sense of the situation and wants to stay in the relationship, may excuse his rage by saying things like; *"He has a very stressful job"*, *"He is having a hard time coping because his boss is riding him too hard"* or *"He's just blowing off steam"*.

These are some ways his game of portraying himself as a victim playing on his partner's sympathy can pay off for him.

Emotionally and Verbally Abusive Behaviors – These behaviors can make a narcissist's partner feel "less than". This has the effect of keeping the partner afraid to act on her own behalf and having confusion about what she even wants. Feeling "less than", in a relationship, is abusive because the victim thinks she is not valued and her feelings are not validated. One tactic, which seems relatively harmless, is questioning her about things she knows very well. It could be something as simple as, "Do you know how to find this address?" Even though she has gone there many times, it makes her feel like he has no confidence in her. As harmless as this may seem, when it is done with the wrong intention it can tear down her self-confidence and self-esteem.

Another verbally abusive behavior is to imply that the partner's work is not as valuable as the narcissist's. For example, if his partner is a teacher, instead of acknowledging that she works hard he might say; *"I don't understand why you need me to help to do "x", you shouldn't be tired, all you've been doing all day is playing with kids"*. Such belittling and disrespectful comments are demeaning and makes her feel unappreciated and powerless.

Verbal abuse also appears as continual criticism and put-downs like when she tries to give her opinion he responds with *"What do you know?"* in a half joking way. So, she goes along with it, because she feels she has no other choice and lets things slide. If this type of abuse is constant, it is hard to push back against because she doesn't want to be fighting with him all the time.

Passive-aggressive swipes, more verbal abuse, are underhanded, more subtle than saying something directly, and can be hidden in something like a backhanded compliment. He shows his disapproval without talking about his disapproval, but the message gets across just the same. For example: if he says, *"You are so beautiful, but why are you wearing that dress"*, he is showing how he feels in an under-handed way.

OTHER EXAMPLES OF PASSIVE-AGGRESSIVE TACTICS ARE:

Guilt tripping is done to manipulate, saying "Ok, I'll do it, I know you're too busy to do that for me".

Sabotaging is undermining someone's plans without confronting them directly. This can be done by giving the wrong information that may lead someone to not accomplish their goal.

Procrastination is a way a narcissist can express his frustration with not wanting to do a task without saying directly, *"I don't want to do that"*. He can delay doing something, just by dragging his feet, or making excuses of why he can't do it at that time. It still gives him cover implying he may do it in the future, but wears his partner down, while she is kept in limbo, waiting.

Sarcasm is similar to the backhanded compliment in passive-aggressive behavior. He says you did something well, but then adds, the word "finally". It is another way to put someone down without overtly criticizing them. Although we all can spot this one, sadly we've heard it too often, nasty things are said, under the guise of, "just kidding". lol

Gaslighting – This tactic messes with your mind. Reality is distorted by his denials of what you know. If you say, *"I mailed the letter"*, he may say, *"No I don't think you did"*. This causes you to begin to doubt yourself. Taken to the extreme, you may begin to doubt your memory, your perception of things, and even feel like you are losing some of your memory. It also keeps you off-balance as all this questioning and doubting can make you confused and disoriented. The narcissist needs you to be in a weaker state, so he can continue to manipulate you.

DIFFERENT WAYS A NARCISSIST WILL GASLIGHT YOU

Denial is a large part of gaslighting, when your partner says that a certain event did not happen.

Distortion is similar to denial and has the same effect. He distorts what you are saying to him about a situation which then causes you to wonder about your own recollection or understanding. They both sow seeds of doubt in your mind.

Blaming is a way of not dealing with your concerns. A way of not validating your feelings. The narcissist is able to avoid criticism by shifting blame onto his partner. A typical scenario might go like this: you say, *"I wish you didn't work so much so we can spend more time together"*. Instead of looking at the positive message that you would like to spend more time with him, his "knee-jerk" reaction is to hear it as a criticism. He might then reply; *"Why are you always blaming me, you know I have to work to provide for us, you're the one who spends all the money shopping."* He might go on to point the finger at you even more, by accusing you of stressing him out just by bring up that topic. A subject such as your life together is a "gold mine" for narcissists. They can use it to play victim, by turning it around on you, saying you are demanding too much of him. It is all calculated to ensure you don't bring it up again.

Projection and Deflecting also have elements of blaming. When the gas-lighter accuses you of doing exactly what they are doing, they are projecting their behavior onto you, to deflect possible criticism. If you ask, *"Why didn't you feed the dog?"* they might say, *"Well, you never feed him on time"*. Whatever their bad habits, if you bring it up to them. they will find a way to project it back on you to deflect criticism. In their mind they are never wrong, so you must be the problem.

Another way they deflect is by going on the offensive. This works to keep you on the defensive, and that's exactly where he wants you. He might say, *"Why are you bringing this up now?" "Can't you see I am stressed out from work, are you trying to hurt me?" "You are not supporting me". You are putting me in a bad mood?".* These tactics can give him the "upper-hand" in your relationship and have you second guessing yourself with this vicious circle game the narcissist plays so well.

Triangulation is when a third person is brought in to make you feel jealous or insecure. It can also make you feel you are in competition with this third person for his affection. This is a clever one, as he gets his ego stroked at the same time it depletes your energy as you are defending yourself.

Contradiction is used to confuse and leave you doubting what really happened. This is done by telling a story in several different ways.

Minimizing is like blaming, and has the same effect of downplaying your concerns and needs. It is usually used to invalidate your feelings by saying you are too emotional or you are exaggerating a situation.

Withholding is a way of keeping you in the dark. It is done by withholding information which results in feelings of confusion and keeping you dependent on him.

Silent Treatment is a deadly one, because we have an innate need for connection. When you are dating and someone ghosts you, they stop communicating and you get the picture pretty quickly that they are not into you. When you are married or in a serious relationship and your husband/partner gives you the silent treatment, ignores you, it can be a big cause for alarm. It also makes you feel you did something wrong and you may begin to doubt yourself. Anytime you are doubting yourself it gives him more control.

WHAT IS HAPPENING AND WHY IS IT HAPPENING TO ME?

Narcissists live in a world of opposites. Because the narcissist wants to keep you in the relationship, he has to make sure you are not feeling good about yourself. He doesn't want you to fulfill your hopes and dreams, because he wants you to be putting all your energy into him. He needs you to keep feeling he is the center of your universe.

Because you are there to continually serve him, he doesn't want you to feel strong enough, to have your own opinions and friends, or to leave him. With this in mind, you will see why he doesn't support your goals for yourself.

It is a bit like a prisoner situation and some have even said a narcissist's partner can develop "Stockholm Syndrome". This is a psychological affectation which sometimes happens when people are held captive. They develop a coping mechanism for their survival where the victim actually identifies with the people who are holding them captive. The victim may even sympathize with their captors and make excuses for them, thinking of their captors as the victim, instead of themselves. This is what I call the "upside down bizarro" world. Knowing the narcissist's mind will give you a glimpse into how a person can be caught up in that world. Once you are aware of all these tactics, you can try a few of your own, starting with the word, No!

JANE'S STORY: GIVING UP ON HER DREAM TO KEEP HER HUSBAND HAPPY

For years, Jane wanted to go back to school. Her husband told her it was out of the question. He could not cope with taking care of their kids while she went to class two nights a week. It was only after she decided to leave him, that she felt strong enough to demand something for herself. Jane did go back to school under his protestations, at first. But, once she was going, she never heard any more about it. Because she finally stood up for herself and insisted on doing it.

You cannot put everyone else's happiness above your own. If you are being manipulated and controlled by a narcissist, it is difficult to assert yourself. When you start to prioritize your own happiness, you may have to fight for what you want and need. But it will be worth it to live an authentic life. You must champion yourself for your own emotional well-being. Your partner will have to go along with it, if you advocate for what you need. If he continues to refuse, then you will know a lot more about how much he is willing to do to make you happy. Remember, you always have the power to make choices for your own happiness.

TAKEAWAYS

- Narcissists are not powerful on their own, all their tactics are to gain your power.
- Because narcissist's tactics are for control, every time you allow him to use his tactics against you, you are losing a bit of yourself.
- Their most powerful tactics are:
  - Love-bombing, charm offense – to get you hooked into the relationship.
  - Gas-lighting – to keep you believing in his superiority, by keeping you off balance.
  - Passive-aggressive comments – to do damage to your self-esteem, without you realizing it. They can be so subtle, well-crafted, and fly under your radar, leaving you not knowing why you are so unhappy.
- You have the power to stop abuse.

"The quality of your life is the quality of your relationships." Anthony Robbins

CHAPTER FIVE

Anatomy of Narcissistic Relationships

Comparing Overt and Covert Narcissists

Let's take a closer look at how these two distinct types of narcissists differ. The select list of narcissistic characteristics described in chapter 3 can be readily seen with an overt narcissistic personality, the "typical narcissist". "Grandiosity" and "arrogance" are considered hallmarks of this type of narcissism. The overt narcissist is not a stranger to most people, as most of us are all too familiar with these people. Where we can be fooled is when we encounter a covert narcissist. But, don't be fooled, those same characteristics may be lurking underneath the surface, just better hidden. During times of stress, you will get a better view of what is hidden beneath his polished surface. They may also have different patterns of behavior. The covert narcissistic partner won't tell you exactly what he wants, as it is part of his control and manipulation to keep you guessing.

COVERT NARCISSISTS

Not all people who exhibit some of these narcissistic traits or tendencies are narcissists. Without being evaluated by a professional clinician, just because he is exhibiting some narcissistic traits or behaviors, no one would be able to say for sure if he is a narcissist. But, beware of the covert narcissist because they are a special breed. Their tactics are subtle. They are stealth players who fly under the radar while their partner does not perceive what they are doing is actually abusive. This means it takes longer for their partner to figure out their game, which allows for maximum damage. They are playing the "long game" and may be keeping their ugliness hidden for years, as long as it serves their purposes. Then when something changes in their relationship, more narcissistic characteristics show up.

This is usually triggered by a stressful event or some type of change in their lives that puts them on the defensive. If they feel threatened then the smooth façade may begin to crack. This allows their partner to begin to see them for who they really are. Also, in covert narcissists, these characteristics can manifest into passive aggressive behaviors, which can pass for a wry sense of humor, or just a snarky comment. If you are on the lookout for narcissistic behaviors, when you spot them, your consciousness will be raised. Seeing what you originally viewed as just difficult behavior, now reveals itself as narcissistic behavior allowing you to view the person behind the mask.

The covert narcissist has been known to string his wife along for twenty or thirty years and then drop her like a hot potato when he sees a better alternative. This is one of the greatest miseries, when a woman must start over after a very long marriage. Having to leave and live without the person she thought she was going to spend her life with might be one of the hardest things she will ever do! The saddest part being, the harder she has worked to fulfill all his wishes, bending to be the image he wanted her to be, the harder it will be for her to start over. Many times this happens in later life, when she is less able to make the changes she would have been able to do as a younger woman.

ANN-MARGARET'S STORY: LIVING A LIFE WITH BLINDERS ON

Ann-Margaret was strictly old school. She had been married for a very long time and relied solely on her husband, Alexander. She even prided herself in not knowing how to balance a check book. Why would she need to, her husband took care of everything? Her whole sense of self was wrapped up in being his wife. They lived in a beautiful home and seemed to want for nothing. Their grown children speculated on the value of that house as it was one of the biggest in their town. They wondered if they would get proceeds from its sale, with their parents getting older.

Every Christmas, he gave her lavish gifts of clothing and luxury vacations. Every year, after all the gifts were opened, everyone piled into one car and would drive over to her husband's secretary's apartment, so he could give her a small gift. Everyone was offered a drink and it all seemed like the secretary was thought of as a member of the family. The whole family went along with it, year after year.

Ann-Margaret never said a word, but you could tell by the expression on her face that she was not excited to be there. Alexander. was a handsome man, well groomed, with an authoritarian demeanor, behind his charismatic smile. No one will ever know for sure if the secretary was his mistress, but what happened next had a more far-reaching effect on Ann-Margaret's life.

Her husband died suddenly; and of course, Ann-Margaret was devastated. But before she had a chance to grieve his death, the reality of what she was left with set in. She found out the beautiful house, she always assumed would

give her security in her old age, was mortgaged to the hilt and
she was left worse than penniless. Even after selling the house,
she still had bills to pay. She had to live with the reality that
he hadn't cared enough to leave her any means of support,
not even life insurance. Having all that debt, and having to
start over left her in a very difficult spot, both physically and
emotionally. Because she had chosen to not know anything
about their financial affairs and possibly his other more per-
sonal affairs, the rest of her life turned out to be the opposite
of the lovely life she imagined it would be.

Things don't get better with a narcissist partner, in fact, they most probably will get worse. Especially as they age when they may become more self-centered and more rigid in their thinking. Remember the mighty oak, how it breaks in a storm, as compared to the bendable bamboo. You cannot heal him and the chances he will get help are not good, either. Overlooking things with a narcissist partner is not a good idea. The sooner a woman sees and accepts the reality of her situation, the sooner she can begin taking control of her life.

Narcissists are Not Emotionally Available

ROMANTIC RELATIONSHIPS AND DIFFERENT
WAYS PEOPLE FORM ATTACHMENTS

Wanting a romantic relationship is very strong in most people. Some of the ways a person's wants and needs when it comes to relationships are influenced have to do with biology, socialization, and psychological factors. One obvious one, comes from what we see in nature, where some animals mate for life for the survival of their species. Bonding with another should provide greater protection, support, and more ways to help us survive. In neurobiology, studies have shown that the brain releases chemicals that aid in falling in love and staying in love.

Psychology tells us our early childhood experiences help us to form our "attachment style". People who have secure attachment styles have healthier relationships. Others, who were not as lucky, have formed insecure attachment styles, resulting in them having trust issues and problems with intimacy.

Our culture, family upbringing, what our friends are doing with their lives all come together to shape the way we think about wanting a romantic relationship. Many people feel inadequate or insecure unless they are "with" someone. I hear many older women, after being married for many years and when their husband dies, expressing an urgent need to "belong to someone". Subconsciously, there are a variety of societal and learned behaviors that influences how we think about the need for a relationship.

Use both your head and heart when making the commitment to have a physical and emotionally intimate relationship. Some questions you may want to ask yourself, but many never do:

1. Do I really know myself?
2. Do I really know what I want?
3. Is he a person of good character, values and morals?
4. How does he treat other people?
5. How does he get along with his family, any red flags there?
6. What does he say about his exes?
7. Does he want the same things I do?
8. Does he make me feel seen and heard?
9. Is there anything about me, he's told me I should change?
10. Does he show kindness, caring and humility? (Yes, you can fall for a "good guy".)

KNOWING THE NARCISSIST'S RELATIONSHIP GAME

You could save yourself a lot of heartache by knowing the typical progression of a relationship with a narcissist. You can't be blindsided when you know what to expect. Having this information is the best way to "narc-proof" your heart!

There are 3 known distinct stages in the narcissistic relationship cycle. These stages are fluid, and this description is meant only as a guideline. Please keep in mind, every relationship is as unique, as the people in them.

THREE MAIN STAGES OF THE NARCISSIST'S RELATIONSHIP CYCLE
1. Idealization leading to love bombing

In the beginning stage of a narcissistic relationship, the narcissist puts his partner on a pedestal. He gives his partner unlimited attention, possibly gifts, compliments and affection. This stage has also been called the "honeymoon" stage, or could even be described as grooming, as the narcissist is saying what he thinks she wants to hear, from what he has learned from listening to her hopes and dreams for the future.

The narcissist will pour on the charm, telling her things like; he has waited all his life for her, or she is the perfect person for him, making her feel she is the most special woman in the world. This can evoke an intense emotional response from her which helps to connect her to him. It not only intensifies feelings, but she feels she is falling in love with him at a very rapid pace.

2. Devaluation

Competitiveness is one of the narcissistic characteristics which can override closeness, as the narcissist must always win to save his self-esteem. This winning at any cost can come out in different ways. As life goes on and the relationship continues, stress can build from almost anywhere. The narcissist does not handle stress well. He has spent his life avoiding anything that might make him uncomfortable. He will project his shortcomings on to her, with the idea if he complains about her first, she will not be able to complain about him.

At some point in the relationship the narcissist will start to cool toward his partner. It is difficult for him to keep up his very complex dance to hide his real true self. Eventually he slips up. I call this "slippage", that is when she gets a glimpse of who he is behind the mask. It might happen for only a few seconds, and not happen frequently, but should be taken seriously. These instances of slippage, if she is paying attention, will seem out of character with the lovely guy she thought he was. She may catch him in a lie, or he may talk badly about an ex. It may also happen more and more as the relationship progresses. If he slips up too much, he may do something so outside of his normal persona, the fear of losing her will kick in. He will apologize, do whatever it takes to keep her involved. But don't be fooled! A true narcissistic person feels no remorse and can never give a meaningful heartfelt apology.

If he starts to think he has lost her, he might try to win her back. He does this with various tactics such as: trying to go back to the "honeymoon stage" or gas lighting by refusing to admit whatever he did didn't happened. He could try to get her to pity him, to get her sympathy, as he tells her how much he can't live without her. He may use any means of bargaining to play on her emotions to take him back. He may even leave and spend the night elsewhere, but in the morning, he returns, with flowers and begs her for forgiveness. He swears it will never happen again.

His partner most probably will fall for it, at first, because she wants to go back to feeling the love they had at the beginning, the warm memories of how they felt during the honeymoon phase. But that doesn't last very long, and the more often this hurting/ apologizing cycle takes place, the less time will be spent in the loving, secure phase. During this stage, as he vacillates back and forth, treating her like a queen and then devaluing her, those "good times" will become more and more elusive, until they are not there anymore and only bickering is left.

When devaluation is fully realized some of the following tactics will be used by the narcissist, as he makes his dissatisfaction with his partner known. He may become *condescending, critical, belittling, finding fault, dismissive,* or *emotionally distant.* He employs these coping techniques to tighten his control. All of this is very puzzling for his partner, as she had been made to feel so loved and wanted.

Manipulative techniques, such as *projecting, a form of gaslighting,* that shifts blame onto her for things that normally go wrong are one of his specialties. At this point, they could be 6 weeks, 6 months or 6 years into their relationship, but he will do this because he can never admit he is wrong and maybe getting ready to go on to stage three, "Discarding". His partner will feel hurt and confused and might question her own worth or role in the relationship.

3. Discarding and Abandonment

In this third and sometimes final stage, the narcissist may end the relationship abruptly or tell his wife/ partner she is no longer needed, without any explanation. He may have just lost interest, decided his partner was not all he thought she was, or have found a new person he feels validates and adores him more. This, of course is the most hurtful phase. Being discarded can be devastating to his partner who feels betrayed and blindsided. Most people have experienced break ups in some form or other and they can be very hard. But, going through a break-up with a narcissist partner is especially cruel, because they will not give a clear understanding of the reason for the break-up or what went wrong. In their mind why should they, they have already moved on.

4. Hoovering

This stage is not a main one and it may or may not occur. This last gasp of their relationship is where the narcissist tries to suck her back in after he has discarded her. This stage must be avoided at all costs. This is where she must cut all ties with him so she is not kept in limbo. The name "hoovering" comes from the Hoover vacuum cleaner.

To make it even more challenging and hurtful for his partner, having been told she is no longer needed, she may have to find a new place to live, a new job, or maybe even leave a country. This pain can be further compounded, especially if she gave up a lot in the beginning to be in that relationship. Because narcissism is such a complex personality disorder, the breakup of a relationship with a narcissist can be a more hurtful and intense process than a normal ending of a relationship or marriage.

This chapter is a warning. Like the forecast of a hurricane or other disasters on its way, it's not enough to know that it is coming. Knowing the different stages can help you decide what to do. If you are already suffering through some of this cycle, knowing what is coming next will give you the power to plan your safe passage through it. You will be able to take action to guard your heart, make plans for your future, how to set yourself up in case you are on your way to stage 3. Friends and family are key to giving you a support system that will allow you to safeguard your physical and emotional wellbeing.

TAKEAWAYS

- Overt narcissists are easy to spot, covert narcissists are not. Watch and listen carefully to find clues to who they really are, behind the mask.
- You cannot have a loving, stable relationship with a person who is emotionally unavailable.
- When making the commitment to have a physical and emotionally intimate relationship, use both your head and heart.
- Shield yourself from further harm by knowing the three main stages of a narcissistic relationship cycle. Do not allow yourself to get sucked back into a relationship by his hoovering.

"Never allow someone to be your priority while allowing yourself to be their option." Mark Twain

CHAPTER SIX

Narcissist's Supply

What is Narcissistic Supply?

The word supply is specifically used to describe the energy and attention narcissists need to prop up their fragile egos. You can use the words, supply and energy interchangeably. It is said, the person who gives him that energy is his supply. If you are a narcissist's supply he will gain that energy, from your attention, affirmation, willingness to go along, and to be controlled by him. He will demand more, for greater control, all to continue to keep up his fantasy of himself.

Narcissists pick people according to how they can give them a continuous supply to support their needs. They are in need of a lot of empathy, someone who will believe them when they are playing the empathy card. If you have high moral values, they know you will not believe their bad behavior and try to find excuses for it. It also tells them you might be willing to work on a relationship for the greater good. They may even test you with certain questions to find out how confrontational you are. They need a non-assertive person to not push back on their authority.

Narcissists have a psychological addiction to the energy they receive from others' reactions to them. They look to others for their reflection, to know how they are seen. The responses from others, elicited through manipulation tactics and bravado, validates their feelings of importance. Feeling important to him means feeling safe.

Supply can come in many forms. Both positive and negative energy feeds him. He thinks; *"I must be important because people are paying attention to me, people are catering to me."* If he can get people to be envious or jealous of him, that is also taken in as usable energy. He gets pleasure and satisfaction from manipulating people, for their response.

At his core, he is so insecure that his facade of superiority must be continually validated through admiration, adulation, and attention. He needs supply, like we need to breathe air or drink water, to keep him from feeling unprotected from hurt. Without that supply, he feels threatened that people will see him for the flawed person he is. If he is viewed by others as strong, superior, invincible, then he feels that way. The worst thing for his ego is for him to be ignored, or criticized. Because they are only pretending to have good self-esteem, they may become jealous of yours. They want to take your confidence away from you, for themselves. The stronger you are, the harder they will come at you to bring you down. They will devalue you to undermine that confidence. This is the answer to all the questions about why he wants you to feel bad and why he cannot be happy for you.

In a romantic relationship, he has a need for total loyalty, with continual expressions of love and support from his partner. In some cases, he tries to get his partner to be jealous of his relationship with someone else, to illicit a negative response. All of that is in service to bolstering his self-esteem and hiding his brokenness.

Knowing both positive and negative feedback from others is consumed by him in the same way should help you understand why he can act so differently toward you even in the same day. One moment he might be tender and loving and the next dismissive and argumentative. It is all part of his agenda for gaining and keeping supply.

How Narcissists Perceive Their Partner's Love

The narcissist loves and feels loved when you are doing the majority of the giving, and showing him love by putting your energy into the relationship. Because he is addicted to being supplied by you, he may keep you feeling like you're on a yo-yo. Keeping you confused with his inconsistent behavior. Inconsistency and control give him a rush.

The "push-pull" tactics, besides keeping his partner off balance, also keeps her trying harder to gain back stability. Without being able to pinpoint what is wrong with their relationship, she may feel she is the problem or not good enough for him. That motivates her to try even harder.

She must continually prove her loyalty by showing her investment in him. Her actions are constantly being evaluated by him, for how loyal and supportive she is to him. Everything is a test. It is exhausting and her mental health can be ruined living in such a conditionally precarious relationship.

Mentally healthy people work hard to enhance their lives for real accomplishments. They want to use their achievements to make their own and others' lives better. Narcissists use other people as an accomplishment, to enhance their own self-narrative. You may be thrown out of his made-up, royal kingdom, if he feel he is not getting the necessary supply from you.

How Narcissists Find their Supply

Did you find your "soulmate" on a dating app? How about in a want ad? Meeting guys that way can be tricky. Remember narcissists are calculating and know that woman who are seeking a partner that way may not have the kind of support system that would bring her the best partner. We all know about internet trolls, but we don't expect the handsome, soft spoken, well groomed, very educated guy to be one. Conversely, you can find narcissists anywhere, so don't rule out a possible narcissist, even if he turns out to be your best friend's brother.

Just be aware from the beginning of meeting someone, you need to try to know as much as you can about him before you decide to trust him with your heart.

Narcissists target women who are vulnerable. Do you feel lonely? Maybe you just got out of a long-term relationship? Are you searching for love? It is easier for him to work his "magic" (how one woman described his hold over her) on someone who has just moved from another city and doesn't know anyone, or someone who may be at a low point in her life. What if he is your boss and already is in charge of a part of your life? Yes, I know, this is not supposed to happen, but it does a lot. And if the office policy is not to date your boss, if you marry him, no one can say a word. Maybe you go to a different department?

He might also be looking for someone who has means and is willing to help him with some projects. Whatever a prospective partner brings to the table, you can be sure the narcissist has an agenda and it is always with an eye to satisfying his needs. Because of their personality disorder, they just can't help making everything all about themselves.

SOME PHRASES TO LISTEN FOR EARLY ON:
> *"I have never felt this way before, about anyone."*
> *"I have waited all my life for you."*
> *"Where have you been all my life?"*
> *"You check every box on my list."*
> *"You are the perfect package."*

If you heard these words, you might question them, especially if he says them to you on the first date! Eek!!!!

It's a beautiful thing to fall in love with an emotionally healthy person. But be cautious, be careful to not go down a rabbit hole with a narcissist posing as a healthy person.

Ways Narcissists Obtain Supply from Others

- Exhausting people's emotional energy
- Exerting their power over them

- Exploiting others to fulfill their needs
- Sexual gratification, but not real intimacy
- Taking pleasure in deceiving to get what they want

How to Avoid Becoming a Narcissist's Supply

Get to know as much about him as you can. Ask him questions and pay attention! If he refuses to answer your questions, or tries to evade them in any way, that is something to watch out for, as well. Of course, in the beginning of your relationship he will show you only his best side, but there are still ways you can be smart to "look before you leap". When you are first dating, it is easy to get swept away, especially when he turns on the charm. Keep your mind free enough to ask yourself questions about this new person.

WHAT DO PEOPLE AROUND HIM, SAY ABOUT HIM?
WHAT DOES HIS FAMILY SAY ABOUT HIM?

Two different families gave me clues I chose to ignore. You must to be willing to be receptive; look and listen carefully. If you don't go into a relationship blindly, you most likely will not be blind-sided later. Many women are so in love, with the idea of being in love, that they choose to ignore warning signs. One family said (talking about both a father and a son), "You know they are difficult, but hang in there, they are worth it". At the time, I thought it so rude, that a mother would say that about her husband and son. I found out later, for myself she was trying to warn me, but by then it was too late.

Years later, when I was introduced to another family, as a prospective girlfriend, the parents' faces told the whole story. They looked like they had just been told someone had died. They were very friendly to me, but if I had paid attention to their initial reaction, my life could have been a lot different. I know this, because I have pictures of these same family members making similar faces at our wedding. Both families knew their sons, but of course couldn't come out and say, *"Don't marry him!"*

DOES HE INTRODUCE YOU TO FAMILY, FRIENDS, AND CO-WORKERS?

Another clue can be found by who he introduces you to. Does he introduce you to his family when it is the appropriate time? Another place to find out more about him is from his co-workers. They know a different side of him than he is showing you. If he doesn't introduce you to co-workers or friends, it is not because he is embarrassed by you, it is because he is afraid, they might "spill the beans" about him. He might also be trying to keep his options open.

WHAT DO PEOPLE OTHER THAN HIS FAMILY SAY ABOUT HIM?

You never went to one office party, and when he said those parties were for office workers only, you took his word for it. Of the many lies he told you it turned out this too was a lie. When you inadvertently met a few people from his office at a conference and they saw your name tag, they questioned you about him, curious to know how he was at home. You could tell they were surprised to hear how wonderful you thought he was. They knew him better than you did.

Is he supportive of the time you spend with your friends, or does he want to keep you all for himself? You may take this as a loving gesture, but it might be for isolation and manipulation to get more supply from you.

How does he talk about his exes? Does he tell you horror stories and play on your sympathy? Does he use derogatory terms to describe other women he has known? If you can put aside the first flushes of becoming addicted to "falling in love" with a narcissist long enough to pay attention, you may just be able to change course and avert becoming a narcissist's supply.

Am I A Narcissist's Supply?

Just as all the power you will ever need is within you at this moment, the same thing can be said for the answers to your questions about your situation. The answers are all there, but sometimes we just don't want to face them. If you are already in a relationship with a person who is making you unhappy, then you are most probably in a toxic relationship. Know that a narcissist only values you for how you enhance and inflate him. To determine if that relationship is with a narcissist, you can never know for sure, but now that you know a lot of the characteristics and tactics, you can begin to evaluate your situation, for your own protection.

Here are some ways you can get a better idea of what is happening in your relationship. If you relate to these questions below, if you say, *"Yes, that's how I am feeling"*, or *"I am experiencing some of the same things"*, then you will know you are in an abusive relationship and it is time to find ways to make a change. I am sure you may have many of your own questions that do not necessarily appear here. These questions are just a starting point, a way to become more aware of unsafe situations in narcissistic relationships. They are in no particular order.

WHAT IS YOUR GUT TELLING YOU?
Go through the following list of questions to see how many may point to a source of your own physical or mental discomfort and pain.

- Do you feel you get nowhere when you try to talk with him about your needs?
- Are you spending too much time thinking of ways to please him?
- Are you worried you are unworthy or not good enough?
- Do you worry about what you will say to him when he comes home?
- Are you emotionally drained just trying to have a meaningful conversation?
- Do you suffer with low energy?
- Are you feeling confused or guilty?
- Are you constantly making excuses for his bad behavior?

- Are you doing so much for others that you have neglected taking time for yourself, time to de-stress?
- Are you in touch with your emotions?
- Are you afraid to ask yourself the hard questions?
- Do you find yourself being comfortable living in a fog, rather than living an intentional life?
- Do you go along with what he wants, all or most of the time?
- Do his goals take precedent over yours?
- Do you suppress your own needs to prop him up?
- Do you care more about his happiness than you do your own?
- Is your partner critical of your personality, physical appearance, or intellect?
- Do you try to change aspects of yourself to please him or to stop his criticism?
- Do you take extraordinary measures to change yourself and is he still criticizing you?
- Are you subjugating your true self?
- Do you lie to yourself and others about your relationship?
- If certain people knew you were unhappy, would they say, "*I told you so*"?
- Are you questioning what you are seeing or hearing?
- Does your partner take responsibility for his own actions?
- When you need an apology, does he start by pointing out that you have done something similar to what you want him to take responsibility for?
- Do you feel unheard or unseen by your partner?
- Does he blame you for anything bad that happens in your relationship, while taking credit for everything good?
- Does he have unreasonable demands and expectations of you?

People's brains are wired for positive connection with others. Especially in a loving relationship, for your peace of mind you need harmony, consistency, being able to count on waking up each morning with the same person. With narcissistic drama you may be caught in a tempest storm, not knowing which way is up. These tactics keep you guessing, off balance, and eventually you lose much of yourself. He needs all your focus on satisfying his needs, because doing his bidding distracts you from knowing what is really happening.

There are hundreds of thousands of women who can relate to what you may be going through. It is shocking to read women's stories of ways their narcissist partners use tactics to manipulate them. You can read 100 stories and they all sound similar. Even more shocking is how many women are still confused by their narcissist's behavior and are unsure if they should keep giving them more and more chances. Some have lived in these unhealthy relationships for 25 years or more.

Being a woman means you already belong to a supportive community. There are so many different ways you can tap into that community, and others for support. Just know, whatever you are going through, you are not alone.

Overlooking the things that are causing harm in your relationship is how you lose yourself. Living an inauthentic life, chips away at your self-worth. Being able to see what your narcissistic partner is doing to manipulate and control you will not only give you a new understanding, a new perspective on why you are feeling the way you do, but will give you the power to start making positive changes in your life.

You don't have the power to change him, but what you do have is the power to change you! Start by doing things to build your self-esteem. The stronger your belief in yourself, the harder it will be for anyone to take advantage of you. Take pride in things you do outside the realm of pleasing him. Do things just for you, things that make you happy! This is how you gain back your power. Taking action when you have a clearer understanding of your situation will put you on the path to self-healing, to begin to discover you, again.

TAKEAWAYS

- You become a narcissist's supply when you give him power over you.
- It is never your fault if he chooses you.
- Narcissists are addicted to the energy, both positive and negative, they gain from others.
- Try to learn as much as you can about a new person before you get into a relationship with them.
- Don't ignore important clues about his intentions.
- Watch and listen to people who know him well, how they react to him and what is said about him.
- The solutions to all problems are already there, you just have to find the strength to face them.
- You don't have the power to change him, but you do have the power to change how you think about him and how you react to his behavior!

"But love is blind, and lovers cannot see." Shakespeare (Merchant of Venice)

CHAPTER SEVEN

What Blinds us to Reality When Falling for a Narcissist?

The Biology and Chemistry of Love with a Narcissist

Is love really blind or is your brain in a fog from all the love chemicals? Love is a complex combination of sociological, psychological, and biological factors. Romantic love is even more complex because it involves a deep connection between two people. The couple can develop a strong emotional bond, through their physical attraction to each other, which gives them the desire to be close, intimate, passionate, and connected. When you are with the person you love you can feel joyful, excited, and even feeling that you are fulfilling your purpose. Romantic love can bring up such strong emotions, you may feel euphoric. Many other feelings can come into play such as: admiration, respect, loyalty, and commitment. Romantic love also may involve a powerful attachment to the person you love and if both partners feel that commitment equally it can bring them much happiness and fulfillment.

You feel these emotions so strongly, because when in love, all those feelings are driven by the chemicals your brain manufactures and sends to your nervous system throughout your whole body. But, when you fall in love with a narcissist, because of his love bombing and other control tactics it becomes an even more heightened experience for you.

We are social creatures and most everyone longs for connection. Through deprivation (isolation) studies we know humans crave connection. Without human connection most people rapidly decline mentally and physically. Deep bonds with people provide us with trusted support systems to maintain our mental and physical health. Older people who have lost many of those connections can live longer, healthier lives by making new friendships and maintaining family ties.

We get health benefits from having a pet. Research shows your blood pressure can be lowered just from petting your cat or dog. We all know how therapy dogs go to hospitals to bring smiles to sick children's faces. That is all about connection and the chemicals your brain makes when a special connection is felt. Good social connections create "feel-good" chemicals in your brain, which helps to give you a sense of well-being.

On the other hand, being in a toxic relationship, not having that positive feedback from the person you feel connected to hurts your mind and body by producing harmful stress chemicals that can lead to many different types of illnesses. That is why a bad relationship is called toxic. It messes with your normal brain chemicals. Your body sends you signals if your relationship is bad for you. If you pay attention to what your body is telling you, you can stay ahead of the game.

To understand a narcissist's power over you, it is important to know how the narcissist uses that need for connection to bind you to him. To keep you invested in a relationship with him, he uses his control tactics to ensure you ignore the signs which might make you want to leave, even when you know you should. It has to do with the chemistry of love which has your body making and releasing pleasure chemicals which literally addict you to the feelings of being in love.

The feeling of falling in love is an extreme reaction to that perceived connection. Your brain releases many different chemicals. It is not just falling in love, it is talking with a loved one, seeing a love one, anticipating seeing a loved one. Just thinking about him can make all those pleasure chemicals begin to flow. The whole first part of the honeymoon phase is setting up the love cycle, which reinforces your enjoyment of being with him and wanting that to continue. His attention and affection become a need rather than just a want for you because of that love cycle of pleasure reward and bonding.

(From Emma's story about Jerry and the Charming Bud-vases from Chapter 4)

> *Emma, had fallen so hard for Jerry, she didn't quite understand it. At first, she wasn't even that interested in him. So, it was difficult for her to figure out how it happened. Yes, he was handsome and charming, but she had thought of him as a friend. But then she thought back to the day when her feelings for him changed.*
>
> *It was the day they were out on a boat, with his son. When she saw how tender he was with the young boy, she felt a shift in her feelings for him. Her brain had been chemically altered and consequently her heart. She knew it, the day out with his son, was the day she fell for him.*
>
> *The feelings she had for him felt like being addicted to a drug. It was intoxicating! They always had so much fun together and she had allowed herself to trust him, depend on him and even plan a future with him.*
>
> *When the realization of who he really was hit her, after seeing those 3 other bud-vases, she knew she had to cut*

it off completely with him. She had to go "cold-turkey" and never see him again, treating that relationship like the addiction that it was. Breaking those powerful bonds, once your brain is altered, it is very difficult and can cause mental, emotional and even physical pain.

The Chemicals that Control Your Feelings

Being in love has a significant impact on the brain. The narcissist plays on those emotions to manipulate you. To experience pain from a narcissist who disregards your feelings has nothing to do with anything you have done. It is all about how your brain responds to various situations that stimulate it.

The more you understand how these love chemicals work, the more insight you will have about how powerful they are at controlling your emotions. You will begin to see how this deep connection you think you have with your partner, actually comes from you *wanting* to be in love and the chemicals your brain releases when you are in contact with the person you love. This is one of the reasons why sex binds you to your partner, because the closer the contact the more chemicals released.

When you are feeling helpless, twisting in the wind, or being reeled back in, you will start to see how this cycle can be dependent on the love chemicals and is used for manipulation by your narcissist partner. This knowledge will help you set boundaries and put you on the path to making better choices.

Many women talk about how powerless and lost they are when finally realizing their narcissist's game, but don't know what to do next. Many blame themselves even though all the abusive behavior is coming from the narcissist. Knowing how your brain functions on the love chemicals can show you how similar your feelings are to being addicted. You will know it is not something you are doing or not doing. Having this insight can help you to begin healing.

How Your Brain "In-Love" is Affected

Memory and learning can be affected by the emotions of love. You may find you remember events differently. It is colored by your emotions, like looking through "rose-colored" glasses. This is one reason gaslighting works better on people who are viewing the world through those feelings-of-being-in-love. They are more vulnerable to persuasion.

Research shows that parts of your brain light up and are more active when you feel you are in love. Those regions of the brain are the ones that have to do with attachment, commitment, motivation, and reward.

Chemicals are made in the neurons in your brain, then they go to various parts of your body. These chemicals are called neurotransmitters, because they carry messages to your brain, glands, and muscles. They control everything that is happening in your body. In your brain, the "love chemicals", when set free, communicate with your nervous system to give you feelings of well-being, pleasure, and bonding. The longer you are in the state of feeling loved and in-love, the harder it becomes to let go of the bond you feel with your partner. Love chemicals do make changes in your brain, but it is thought they are not permanent changes. More research needs to be done.

There are very real consequences from receiving love and then having that love withheld, as the narcissist plays his power games. When love is withheld those love chemicals will not be flowing. This is equal to no feelings of pleasure, bonding, or well-being. Neurotransmitters also communicate with muscles and glands. So, if you are in an unhealthy relationship, where you feel like you are on an emotional rollercoaster, you may also feel bad physically. Your muscles might ache, you could be losing sleep, even your digestive system can be upset. Our bodies feel emotional pain through the brain-body connection carried out by the neurotransmitter chemicals. The brain-body connection is where your mind influences your body and the body influences your mind in a feedback loop. That is why you should always trust your gut. Our bodies don't lie, even when our brains might want to hide the truth.

A Closer Look at the "Love Chemicals"

It is no wonder so many people spend so much time, energy and money trying to find love. People want to find that one perfect person who will make their heart flutter. What they don't realize is all those feelings of love come from chemicals made in their own brains. That is why you may feel you are walking on air. Think of all the songs, books, poems, and movies that have been inspired by those feelings involved with being in love. The high you get from being in love is different from any other! Knowing this helps to explain how those feelings can be so captivating, all-consuming and used to manipulate you by a narcissist.

Oxytocin is known as the love chemical for its role in forming bonds. It is released in your brain when you physically touch someone. This may be why people shake hands or hug when they greet, to form social connections. It is strongly associated with romantic love and is released when hugging, kissing, and intimate love making. It helps to bind you to your love interest. It also helps you with empathy and putting trust in people, it can make you feel at peace. Oxytocin is even released when you hug yourself, and also is known to be released when you put other pressure on your body like sleeping under a weighted blanket. Some people swear by it. That may be why babies stop crying, feeling secure when swaddled in a blanket like a burrito. It is good to remember, that a hug can do so much good. Oxytocin can also reduce stress, lessen anxiety and bring a sense of calm to your life.

Dopamine is also known as a love chemical because it is a part of your brain's reward cycle. Dopamine is associated with being in love because it is released even when we are simply thinking of a person we love. It also is involved with feelings of pleasure, excitement, or motivation. This is a strong one and it plays a big part in addiction. Dopamine is also involved in the pleasure of exercise, eating, and social interactions.

Endorphins are usually associated with sports and a "runners high". They also have the ability to kill pain and put you in a good mood, even make you euphoric. They are released under different situations. They are considered a part of this group of love chemicals because they add to your sense of well-being, giving you the happiness of being in a romantic relationship.

Adrenaline is also a familiar chemical, but it is not a neurotransmitter like the others. It is part of the body's "flight or fight" response and is made in the adrenal glands. It works in your body when you are under stress, by increasing your heart rate, making you sweat, and even giving you the feeling of having butterflies in your stomach. That feeling happens when you see the person you love, usually at the beginning of falling in love.

Serotonin is made in your brain to regulate behavior and is thought of as a "feel-good" chemical. It gives you a reward, like the feeling when you eat chocolate. Eating chocolate is a pleasurable experience because serotonin is released in your brain when the chemicals from chocolate are present in your bloodstream. That may be the reason we give "Chocolates" on Valentines' Day. Serotonin plays a role in social interactions and in being in love. When serotonin levels fluctuate up and down in love, you can experience emotional highs and lows. When serotonin levels stay low, you can feel anxious and even depressed.

Out of the five love chemicals outlined above, there are three that are involved at every level of being in love. All these chemicals are natural, made by your brain and are a good thing for you when in a healthy relationship. They function to help you fall in love and keep you committed to a loving relationship.

Understanding the roles of these powerful chemicals in a healthy relationship can show you the possibility of how you can be hurt when a narcissist is falsely taking you on a fantasy ride for control and manipulation. The following shows the role each of the three main love chemicals plays to fuel each stage:

Physical Attraction Stage
- Oxytocin is considered "the cuddle hormone" as it promotes closeness and attachment.
- Dopamine deals with desire and anticipation.
- Serotonin regulates emotions of attraction and attachment.

Falling in Love Stage
- Oxytocin is also considered the "love hormone", creating a sense of connection between partners.
- Dopamine rewards you with pleasure when you are with him, which motivates you to want to keep being with him.
- Serotonin, because it regulates moods, can give you feelings of happiness and well-being when you are together, or when you are not together might have you obsessing over the need to be together.

Sexual Activity Stage
- Oxytocin is released during sex and plays a role in trust, bonding, attachment, intimacy, and relaxation.
- Dopamine is increased during this stage. It is a part of the reward system, giving feelings of pleasure which motivate you to want to repeat this stage.
- Serotonin decreases stress.

Addiction Stage
- Oxytocin can help out in this stage, as it is a feel-good chemical and can limit the feelings of a need for substance abuse. But you might get addicted to feeling too good.
- Dopamine reinforces pleasure and rewards behavior that can cause you to want to repeat that behavior.
- Serotonin, when you are in a compromised state, can drop to lower levels which can affect your mental health.

Love as Compared to an Addiction

We can compare being in love to being hooked on a drug because of the powerful emotions we feel that keep us bonded to our narcissistic partner, even when we know it is unhealthy. Being addicted to feelings of love produced from your brain chemicals is comparable to being addicted to mind altering chemicals that give you similar feelings of pleasure and euphoria.

Both change your brain chemistry by working on the brain's reward pathways. This makes you want to repeat that behavior by associating it with pleasure. Both love and addiction initiate a strong desire, an urge to keep up this behavior. Because of how strong these feelings are, they can be difficult to resist. Both can change your behavior, as being in love can change your priorities and influences how you make decisions. Chemical dependency can cause significant behavioral changes as the addict prioritizes their need for the drug. In a narcissistic relationship, we know only too well, how women change their priorities and behaviors just to please their partners.

Both can lead to negative influences on your life. You may destroy other relationships, healthy support systems and your own well-being. When being in love or being drug addicted no longer gives you that emotional boost, you suffer withdrawal symptoms. Withdrawal symptoms come from a lack of good brain chemicals which can impact your mood, stability, ultimately causing anxiety or sadness, as well as physical symptoms.

When your narcissistic partner withdraws his affection, you are left confused. You have been through powerful experiences, chemical changes in your brain that have bonded you to him and now you are left to figure it all out on your own. It can be as difficult and bewildering as having to deal with a chemical dependency. If you can relate to and find yourself suffering or struggling with some symptoms of withdrawal from a narcissistic relationship, you may want to seek a professional mental health clinician to help you sort through your feelings.

THE DARK SIDE OF ROMANTICIZED LOVE
During childhood, fairy tales give us a false picture of "true love". Little girls grow up believing they will meet their "prince" someday. Movies and songs are written to portray a very rare, overly romanticized version of love. By romanticized, I mean we are believing there is such a thing as a perfect love. Since people are not perfect, it is unrealistic to think we can find love that is perfect. This kind of love would

be one that never changes, takes no work, with couples who always agree, and have perfect endings. The idea of perfect love sets us up for failure. We all know there is no such thing. But, by the time we find out it is beyond our reach, it might be too late. By then, we may have been caught up in the dream of the perfect partner and perfect life. It all has to do with managing expectations and being grounded in reality. That is the opposite of what we are led to believe as little girls.

There is a saying that fits this situation well. "Don't let the perfect be the enemy of the good". It applies to many situations in life, but when we are eliminating people to date because they don't measure up to the fairy tales, we may just miss a chance for real happiness.

My Cousin Sandy has always said: "G-d damn Walt Disney for all those "Princess" movies." She and I have spent hours trying to figure out how we went so wrong when choosing perspective mates. It can influence little girls' expectations of their future perfect relationship. In my own life, because my parents never allowed me to see them fight, I was only allowed to see an unrealistic view of marriage. When I experienced my first fight, I didn't know what to do. I thought the marriage was over. I had no tools to deal with reality.

These fairytales influence women to still be waiting for their prince to come, swoop them up, and carry them off, to live "happily ever after." The narcissist is like a chameleon, slithering around learning your dreams so he can make you think he is the one to fulfill them.

Our willingness to believe the fantasy makes us vulnerable to the narcissist's advances. We are willing to take a chance even if there are red flags all over the place. The narcissist is happy to be our "prince" for a while, until it stops working for him.

I know women fall for this fantasy, from the thousands of comments on social media. It amazes me what a large response the online workshops get by promising to give you the power to manifest your "prince" and a perfect relationship. There are so many of them offering programs promising to teach you methods of changing your thinking or how you look to find "the man of your dreams". There are scammers out there even offering you ways of finding your "soul-mate".

There are wonderful relationships and marriages that have stood the test of time, but those people are very lucky to have found each other; and both had to be willing to work hard for what they have achieved. If you are being "love bombed", and it seems "too good to be true", it probably is. Use a healthy dose of skepticism until you get to know the person well enough to know if his feelings for you are genuine.

TAKEAWAYS

- Romantic love with a narcissist is heightened emotionally because the narcissist uses love bombing and other control tactics to bond with you and bind you to him.
- The very powerful "love" chemicals that are made and released in your brain are what give you the feelings of being in love, but can also cause many changes in your own personality by affecting mood, commitment, and priorities.
- Romantic love can be compared to being addicted to a substance because of how it makes you feel and how hard it is to deal with symptoms of withdrawal when it is gone.
- If you are in an unhealthy relationship, it is never your fault. Chemicals and society have played roles leading you into and keeping you in that relationship.

"If you change the way you look at things, the things you look at change." Wayne Dyer

CHAPTER EIGHT

Spotting Red Flags!

How Prevalent are Narcissistic Relationships?

While doing research for this book, I came across many Facebook groups that were formed and populated by people who not only want to talk about their abuse by a narcissist, but were looking for support and help from fellow victims. I was surprised not only to find so many different groups, but so many people in each of these groups.

You will find some listed here to give you an idea of how prevalent this type of relationship is. Ignoring a narcissist's "red flags" can be dangerous to your heart and well-being. It emphasizes the amount of hurt and damage people are experiencing when in relationships with narcissists.

It is heartbreaking to read numerous stories recounting the hideous things their partners have done to them, to hook them, then treat them badly, dump them, and wanting them back, which leaves a trail of destruction. (All the phases of the "Narcissistic Relationship Cycle".) Too many of the stories follow the same pattern, reinforcing that narcissism is a very real personality disorder, a life-altering situation, and the patterns are knowable. It also shows hundreds of thousands of people who ignored the red flags that might have saved them from getting into a narcissistic relationship in the first place.

Seeing red flags is important. You can make the analogy of buying a house with a big crack in the wall to marrying a narcissist without looking beneath the surface. If you disregard the crack in the wall, you may end up with buyer's remorse, jacking up the whole house to fix the foundation. With a narcissist, if you don't learn who he really is before marriage or getting into a committed relationship, you run the risk of missing his cracks beneath his surface that indicate he has a faulty foundation, too! The main difference is the house can be fixed, but a narcissist usually cannot.

With all that is known about this personality disorder, you have a roadmap to catch them at their game and put a stop to it. Nothing is fool-proof, because many narcissists are very skillful and use stealth tactics to ensnare their partners, but at least you can be armed before you go into battle.

There seems to be an ongoing almost daily battle, coming from a stream of imposters, online, or on your phone. Without seeing the red flags popping up about their amazing offers, you might be scammed. Armed with information about their intentions you are able to fend them off without being harmed. Similarly, the narcissist, with love bombing and other tactics, is offering you a "too good to be true" vision of your future with him. To protect yourself from both the scammer and narcissist, you must know how to spot the red flags and to do it at the outset, before you get in too deep with either one.

The difference between the scammer sitting at his computer on the other side of the world and the handsome charismatic narcissist sitting across the table from you is the scammer wants your money and possibly your identity; the narcissist might want all you have, but that's not enough for him. In the process, he also has the ability to break your spirit and your heart!

NUMBER OF PARTICIPANTS IN FACEBOOK GROUPS
ABOUT NARCISSISTIC RELATIONSHIPS (2024)
1. Wives of Narcissists 2.4 K
2. Christian Wives of Narcissist Husbands 1K
3. Narcissists: Surviving Toxic Relationships 1.1K
4. Dealing with the Narcissist 187K
5. Narcissist 13K
6. N.P.D. Survivors 77K
7. Narcissists and Toxic People's Memes 3K
8. Narcissistic Boyfriend 16K
9. Male Victims of Female Narcissists 8.9K
10. Narcissistic Abuse and Trauma Recovery 36K
11. Steps to Healing After Narcissistic Abuse 75K
12. Women's Support Group for Narcissism 19K
13. Narcissist Abuse Recovery 47K
14. Daughters of Covert Narcissistic Mothers 43
15. My Abusive Narcissistic Family 55K
16. Victims of Narcissistic Abuse 34K
17. Surviving Narcissist's Emotional Abuse 42K
18. Daughters of Narcissist Mothers 25K
19. Understand the Narcissist 6.7K
20. Living with and Divorcing a Narcissist 9.9K

These 20 groups were randomly chosen out of a much larger number I found on Facebook. You might imagine that these Facebook group's numbers are just the tip of the iceberg, as there are many more groups on so many different platforms. This snapshot in time gives you an idea of how pervasive this problem is. How many people are trying to manage, deal with, figure out, get out, not be sucked back in, and rebuild lives from the heap of rubble that is left after being in a narcissistically abusive relationship. The pattern of abuse and destruction is not just confined to the two people involved in the relationship.

There are children, grandchildren, and a legacy of shattered relation-ships that also merit consideration. How many of those shared stories in those groups involve tremendous cruelty and indifference? How many write about still being in a fog years after the relationship ended, where they are asking the group for advice about taking him back? And every reply is a resounding "NO" because the group seems to have the same shared experiences. While wanting revenge, as so many do, is a valid emotion, it is the wrong way to go. If he cheats on you, he will continue to cheat on his mistress. There is karma in that. You don't need to worry about exacting revenge, he is already cursed be-cause he can never find true love. Your revenge is to live your best life.

Don't ignore red flags, take action. What are some actions you can take to ensure you are not making yourself powerless against the narcissist's tactics. First, how you respond when you spot a red flag depends on where you are in your relationship, how far along you are and what is the current situation. You also want to evaluate how important a red flag this is in terms of, is it a deal breaker or just a small slip.

- The first thing to do is be patient, you don't want to jump fast before you understand what is going on.
- No response is a response, if you choose to make a mental note of a red flag and put off dealing with it until it comes around again. But there are times doing nothing should not be an option.
- Do not be complacent in your life, it is yours. Complacency equals complicity in abusive situations.
- Question him about what just happened or something uncharacteristic you observed about him. Always do this in a non-threatening way, because he could close down or come back at you with twice the energy.
- Listen carefully to be sure to get the whole story, or see his complete reaction.

- If something is threatening to you, or disrespectful, always stand up for yourself. Tell him you don't appreciate what he did or said in a firm, but neutral way.
- If his answer to your question is a tactic such as gaslighting, passive-aggressive swipes or projection, saying it was your fault, or he didn't mean it that way, you can calmly say I don't accept that. Stand your ground, even if it looks like he doesn't hear you, say what you want anyway. He is listening even if it doesn't seem that way and it is good for you to have a voice.
- If his answer is no answer, or he ghosts you, then you will have your answer. You will know what you thought about the red flag you observed was well-founded. This will not only protect your self-esteem, but will show him you are paying attention and are on to his game.
- If the dragon comes out, then you will have an even better idea of who he is and how he feels about you and your relationship, as long as you don't make excuses for his behavior.

Remember, it is your life. You are not the problem and never have been the problem. If anything, you have been too empathetic, too kind, too forgiving to a person who cannot appreciate your goodness. He is not your problem to fix, because he is the only one who can fix himself. And, if he could have done that, he probably would have done it a long time ago.

What Specifically are Red Flags?

Red flags are things you should see, but sometimes don't. Perhaps you make up excuses for what you have seen, because you don't want to believe what you saw was true. Even if we see red flags, we may dismiss them as normal behavior. Humans are very adaptable, bad behavior if experienced often enough, will become normalized.

The term red flags can be used in different situations. When there is road construction and an actual red flag is displayed, you use caution slowing down and getting ready to stop. We use red to signal danger and in a relationship with a narcissist, when you witness known characteristics or control tactics, you should see a neon sign flashing on his forehead, "danger ahead".

In friendships, you recognize a red flag when the relationship is one-sided and you find yourself doing all the work. Maybe you are the one who always does the planning and the other person seems to be going along for the ride. If times get hard and that person is not there for you, you would wonder what kind of friend are they? If your friend is constantly criticizing you or caught telling lies about you, then you know they are not your friend. If you feel emotionally exhausted after spending time with them, or don't feel they are interested in you, you would not continue that friendship.

Why is it you are great at spotting money-pit type houses, scammers, and false friends, but go to pieces when it comes to romantic relationships? Why don't the warning bells go off when a narcissist is nearby? There are many factors that go into the answer for this. Why do you let your guard down? Why are you willing to let them into your life without a thought for your own safety?

Many strong emotions and intentions come into play when love is involved and the deeper you are in the relationship, the more invested you get; the more time that passes, the harder it is to leave a narcissistic relationship.

Being vigilant and reading the signs can go a long way to getting a handle on your situation. All this being on guard and having good information doesn't sound sexy or romantic. But it is also not sexy or romantic if you find yourself in a relationship with a person who is not who they portrayed themselves to be. You could wake up one day and realize, *"this is not the same person I thought I married!"*

All narcissistic characteristics we've discussed in this book are red flags. But there are other behaviors and tells to watch for because they might be easily overlooked. There are demeaning expressions meant to be negative toward you or women in general that you might overlook because they seem harmless. They might be things that some people would call "locker room talk", or a "white lie". Other harmful talk or acts may be overlooked just because they happened in a split second and you missed that moment when his mask slipped, indicating your Mr. Right, might be Mr. Not-So-Right. Many red flags are deliberately overlooked because you are unwilling to confront him or have a fight with him. He knows this and letting something important slide will just work against you, as these kinds of things pile up to hurt you at a later time. Some narcissists are so effective in their use of tactics against their partners they are able to get their partner to completely give up on having a say in their own lives. Don't ever give up on who you are.

What is Your Narcissistic Red Flag Trigger?

Finding that one thing, your personal red flag. The one thing that jolts you into finally realizing who they are. The narcissistic trigger! It can be an action or something as small as just one word, but you will know it when you see or hear it. Everyone has a different "tipping point". Something that gives you the insight you need to begin to seriously deal with your narcissist partner's bad behavior. When you witness that behavior, you will have the clarification you need to set boundaries and know you will be able to keep them.

In two separate situations, with many years in-between, under completely different circumstances, I was able to get the clarity I needed to move on, with no regrets.

The first one happened after I arrived on the other side of the world, after a bad breakup. I knew I had done the right thing to leave, there was no other choice, but my heart had not yet caught up with that decision. One day, I had to call my ex. The woman he had cheated with, answered the phone. He and I talked for a bit and then I decided to ask him a question.

I said, *"This is a hypothetical question, it will not happen, but I was wondering, if I said, I was arriving back there in two days, would you come to the airport to pick me up?"* To my surprise, he answered immediately. He didn't answer my specific question, but matter-of-factly said, *"I'd throw the 'bitch' out!"*

That was enough for me. Hearing him refer to the woman he had chosen over me, in that way, was proof enough I had made the right decision to leave. That was the defining moment that allowed me to forget him and never look back!

Years later, I met a man who seemed very nice. But, when I heard him refer to a situation with a woman, describing her as a stray dog he let in and couldn't get rid of, that was enough for me to experience déjà vu.

It is worth taking a minute to think about why these two situations would have felt the same. Have you experienced these kinds of moments of clarity? What do you think would be your moments of clarity, your line in the sand? What boundaries do you have for other people's behavior? If you have boundaries, behaviors you will not tolerate from others, then it is much easier to say no to people who could potentially hurt you. For me, demeaning language toward women and being lied to are big red flags. Have you thought about what your boundaries might be?

How to Spot a Liar

Here are some typical physical signs that can be seen when a person is lying:

- The eyes have it! Eyes are said to be the windows to the soul. There are several tells if you watch a person's eyes. Watch to see if they look you in the eye when they are talking to you.
- Do their eyes dart back and forth?
- Do their eyes move up, as if they were trying to recall something, but then look down and to the right when they are lying?
- Their face might go pale as the blood flowing through small blood vessels near the skin surface are constricted due to fear of being found out.

- Breathing heavier is also a response to the stress of doing something you know is wrong.
- Veins on the side of their neck may be visible and pulsing as the heart is speeded up due to flight or fight hormones from anxiety.
- Sweating of the forehead.

Narcissists Are Too Good at Lying

Lying is a red flag, but you cannot catch narcissists lying from the above tells. Those are for people without NPD. Law enforcement professionals are trained to watch for some of those typical signs that are giveaways when a person is lying. There are over 20 different behavioral changes that show someone is lying. The things they are trained to look for you probably won't see when a narcissist is lying.

Sweating, nervousness, having a pale face, or breathing heavier than normal don't usually happen with a true narcissist. They don't have a conscience, or enough self-awareness to care if they are lying. Lying must first register in the brain as abnormal to produce the physiological changes in the body. Narcissists lie like breathing air; it is not out of the ordinary for them to lie to accomplish their agendas or just because they feel they deserve to do it.

When you were a child, you were probably told not to lie and especially not to lie when you are looking someone in the eye. That is considered a "bold-faced" liar. This is thought to be especially bad because it signals a person who can lie with ease and not think about the consequences. That is a narcissistic tell! When you catch a person lying while looking you directly in your face, possibly believing his own lies, then that is a red flag that he may be a narcissist.

Narcissists Will Paint Themselves as Victims

Don't fall for stories about being victimized by a person or situation. Ask questions about the situation, to find out if the story is true. Narcissists will claim they are victims to get your attention or gain sympathy. When a person is complaining that they are a victim in a situation of their own making, this red flag warrants attention. If a person is truly a victim, the situation cannot be of their own making. The very definition of being a victim is it must come from outside a person's control, where someone or something hurt or damaged them. Narcissists will prey on your good nature, portraying themselves as victims for your sympathy. And they will get their next supply by lying about you.

Unexplained Events Can Be Red flags
MARY'S STORY: WEDDING BELL BLUES

On Mary and George's wedding day, the sun was glinting off the water, as they stood in front of the minister on a beautiful promontory, with a small group of family members around them. They wanted an informal wedding because they were each married before. George decided to limit the wedding party to only close family.

After the wedding they were having lunch in an old Victorian cottage, set in a remote spot, with exquisite foliage. They told their guests to order off the menu, so everyone could have what they wanted.

As the waitress came around taking orders, Mary was having trouble deciding because everything looked so good. Just as she was about to decide, George slapped the back of her hand. She was stunned! It was so unexpected and out of the realm of how she thought of her precious new husband. She just let it go, not allowing it to spoil their day. She never mentioned it to him or to anyone, pretending it didn't happen.

Too bad Mary didn't understand the implications of what she had just experienced. If she had known how important it was to make note of his slippage, this red flag, it could have given her an opportunity to gain valuable insight into George's personality disorder. Maybe, if she hadn't chosen to ignore it, she might not have felt so blind-sided when four years later George announced he wanted a divorce just because he didn't see a future with her.

George was just being his true self, unable to empathize with Mary. She was so excited on her wedding day; she couldn't concentrate on what she wanted for lunch. His lack of patience and awareness allowed him to show his dissatisfaction with her in such an unexpected and inappropriate way. The sheer act of doing something physical to her, chastising her for such a small thing on their special day, should have been a big red flag! This is the type of behavior that should be questioned.

The longer you allow yourself to be taken in by the narcissist, apologizing for his bad behavior, and discounting your own emotional reactions, the more sense of yourself you lose. It also becomes harder and harder to admit you are in an abusive relationship. Time also takes a toll in your ability to take action. It is necessary for you to stop his abusive behavior, but if you have invested so much of yourself you may feel too broken to move forward to help yourself.

Ever catch your husband or boyfriend on the phone with someone but when you ask him about it, he gives an answer that just doesn't add up? What about when he comes home from work and insists, he must take a shower before he can even give you a hello hug? Has he made rules for you, like his job is so stressful he needs some time to unwind in peace, before he can talk with you? What is really going on? These are the kinds of things that should stand out as red flags. Unusual events or behavior should not be swept under the rug. They are telling you something is going on.

In Mary's story about the "Vintage Black Dress", if she had followed the question to its conclusion of why their photo was not included in the "Who's Who" section of the program, she may have gotten some clarity. Instead, she took this incident at face value and thought "How nice, they thought she was his mistress". She might have found out it was her husband who stopped the printing of that photo. He may have done this to continue to lie to his actual mistress about his wife. Most cheating husbands play down their relationship with their wives to the women they are cheating with. Saying things like: *"She doesn't understand me"* or *"We don't sleep together anymore."* They lie to their mistresses, too. They try to make their infidelity more acceptable to themselves and others. He may have been hiding his wife so some people wouldn't even know he was married. That might have been the same reason he refused to wear a wedding ring. Cheaters like to keep their options open.

TAKEAWAYS

- Learning to spot red flags early is the best way to protect your heart.
- Online forums indicate hundreds of thousands of people are damaged by narcissistic abuse. These groups exist for partners of narcissists to tell their stories of destruction, to find out they are not alone and hopefully get answers to their questions.
- Narcissists are expert liars. Don't take things at face value until you know the person you are dating is not a narcissist.
- Unexplained events, those things that just don't feel right, or don't make sense are red flags.
- If red flags appear in a committed relationship, you need to question what is happening. It is your life, too and you want to take an active role in it.

"Childhood should be carefree, playing in the sun; not living a nightmare in the darkness of the soul." - Dave Pelzer

CHAPTER NINE

What's Childhood Got to do With It?

Understanding the Impact of Childhood Trauma

This quote is written by a survivor of childhood abuse. It shows the contrast between what a normal childhood should be and what so many children didn't have growing up in a dysfunctional family where one or more caregivers were emotionally unhealthy. It should be a reminder that children need protection. They need nurturing by growing up in a safe and loving environment. Children are not as resilient as people would like to believe. It is a shame and brings much sadness to know that parents, while they want the best for their children may not understand or know how to provide that. They may be so young and inexperienced, possibly dealing with their own demons. That is why it is important for dysfunctional families to seek family counseling. This is a big problem when only one spouse wants to go and the other refuses.

Also, too many parents cannot recognize when they are traumatizing their children because abuse was normalized by their own childhood experiences. Parents do not realize that anger comes from feelings of shame, injury and insecurity. Anger can also be shown to a child, by disapproval, impatience and lack of feeling. These are not things we normally associate anger with, but they can be just as damaging.

An example of generational abuse would be when: parents hit their child out of fear that if they don't, their child may grow up to be spoiled. There are too many misconceptions about childrearing because of past poor childrearing. It was not that many generations ago, when the motto, "spare the rod, spoil the child" was uttered in most households. They really believed that was part of their parental responsibilities. Parents thought the worst thing was to raise a child who was lazy or wouldn't "amount to anything". Parents were unaware that children's emotional health needed to be cared for. We have now learned if the child's emotional needs are not met, they may end up out of touch with their own feelings and the feelings of others. Over time, repeated psychological injuries become cumulative and have a greater impact. As adults their inner child will continue to relate in relationships as they did as children, trying to resolve unresolved problems from childhood. This can place an almost insurmountable barrier to getting to a loving relationship between a parent and their adult children. They may both be suffering from a form of PTSD, being thrown back into those childhood patterns of behavior and shutting down, rather than resolving things as adults.

Childhood trauma is any form of harmful experiences suffered by a child during their formative years which is emotionally painful or destressing. It can be a one-time event, like a car accident, or a series of abuses that put undue stress on the child's emotional development. During childhood trauma, children do not have the understanding yet to know what they are going through, so instead of developing coping mechanisms, they can experience dissociation to try to deal with whatever is happening. This is when they can lose touch with their own feelings, their sense-of-self. It can have a significant effect on their mental, physical and emotional well-being throughout their lives. It can affect their ability to regulate their emotions and to cope with stress. It is important for anyone who experienced childhood trauma to seek help from a mental health professional. Only they are qualified to help someone do the work to be able to heal and recover.

Childhood trauma affects each child differently according to their own unique qualities, the type and severity of what they experienced.

Ways a Child's Emotional Development is Affected by Dissociation

Dissociation is a response to a trauma which can impact emotional development and how emotions are experienced and expressed. During dissociation, a person disconnects from their thoughts, feelings and emotions to cut off pain. A child can also shut down when they are not able to process their emotions. Dissociation happens in childhood trauma more often than you would think. Indifference is the product of dissociation. When a child is only partially in touch with their own emotions and cannot relate to others' emotions, indifference is what is felt. You can see the link between childhood trauma and the characteristics of narcissism, with lack of empathy and indifference being two of the main ones.

Types of Childhood Trauma

Any one of the following events experienced by a child can cause childhood trauma:

Assault of any kind; sexual abuse, neglect, being a witness to violence, shaming, betrayal, constant criticism, unrealistic parental expectations, and family separation.

This is not a comprehensive list. It is included here to point out some possible childhood abuses to raise awareness of their serious effects. For example: some people may not realize how much damage bullying and constant criticism can do or how damaging living in a dysfunctional home can be.

Most all personality disorders can be attributed to childhood circumstances. Here are some emotionally unhealthy behaviors people who have experienced trauma may exhibit. Childhood trauma impacts people in different ways. It can contribute to the likelihood of these outcomes, either to a person becoming a narcissist or to a person who may become the partner of a narcissist.

The Emotional Impact of Childhood Abuse on an Adult

- **Needy** - People-pleaser, overwhelmed easily, doesn't comprehend other's boundaries, can be codependent.
- **Avoider** - Workaholic, over-thinker, suffers anxiety or panic attacks, a perfectionist, be hyperactive.
- **Socialization** – Addicted to drama, struggle with lack of identity, have negative view of themselves, difficulty connecting.
- **Depression** – Difficulty in taking action, feeling stuck, isolated, numb, shut down.

CLARA REMEMBERS HER CHILDHOOD ABUSE

My first recollection of being an unhappy child was when I was about 5 years old. My mother had taken an old umbrella that was already broken, stripped off the fabric and metal spokes and would hit me with the metal end of the umbrella stick, the part that held the spokes onto the wooden stick. I remember running away from her and sliding under my bed to try to avoid the beating. But she always found me, and was able to beat me around my legs. I was a very stubborn child and even at that young age, after I dried my tears, I would come out of my room and say to her, "Thank you, that's just what I needed". I don't remember that going on too long. But I was constantly told I was different and difficult. My mother also

*told me the reason they were older parents was because
they waited nine years to have me. According to her, my
father didn't want to have a child, wanted to have her
full attention all for himself. I never saw him in that way.
I could tell he loved me; he was always so proud of me.
But I had no cuddly experiences with my father, no hugs.
In those days it was thought that a man might be turned
on by his daughter, so he kept his distance. My parents
never hugged me, like people do today. My family believed
all physical contact was supposed to be kept for grownup
romantic love.*

What Role does Childhood Play in Becoming a Narcissist?

Research teaches us there are 3 main ways a child can grow up to be a narcissist. The first one is called nature, because a child is born with certain character traits. If a child is overly sensitive it can make interacting socially more difficult for him. The second is nurture because it has to do with how his behavior was treated. If he was overly praised or harshly criticized, either extreme can lead to narcissistic traits. The third is also nurture depending on his childhood homelife experiences. If, he grew up in a dysfunctional home with one or more toxic parents, he learned how to be like them because they were his earliest role models. Trauma during childhood is thought to play a large role in creating narcissists, as well.

Childhood trauma impacts the development of the child's personality. It can lead to low self-esteem, acting out, feelings of insecurity, and feeling "less than". This manifests itself in unhealthy coping mechanisms developed to ensure they will not suffer hurt again. In NPD, these coping mechanisms become tactics the narcissist uses against you in a relationship.

It is not always an event which harms a child. Being overly coddled can mean they haven't developed coping mechanism to handle criticism. In an extremely patronizing home, children may not be expected to take responsibilities for their actions or show empathy for others. Parents who concentrate on smoothing out the path in front of their child, never teach their child how to navigate a rough road.

5 Developmental Levels of Relationship Readiness on the Path to Emotional Maturity

These levels always go in this order. Children must work through each stage, level by level to continue to mature emotionally.

1. **Functional Level** – The basic level, can do all the things they need to do to survive in the world, but hasn't yet realized that the people around him matters. Still narcissistic.

2. **Rules and Regulations** – They have matured enough to know the meaning of why we have rules and are living by them. This allows them to get along better in the world without getting hurt. This would begin at the time the child starts to go to school. They are in the process of learning socialization.

3. **Engages with Others According to Values** – This is the level where a narcissistic personality disorder may be formed. This level is the beginning of a foundation of values and principles. If a trauma happens in this stage, the child may dissociate from this process of emotional maturation and cannot complete this third level.

   They will develop their own values, but cannot feel other people's pain or see other people's values. They have trouble separating other people's feelings from their own. Because they are not able to empathize with others, other people's actions only make sense in the context of an extension of their own thinking. They are unable to set aside their ego to see another person out of their "frame" of *"what can you do for me?"* This means they will have difficulty forming true "give and take" adult relationships. They are stuck in level 3.

4. **Empathy** – Recognizing that other people have values and principles and honoring other people's emotional needs, values, and principles. Once in this level, they are considered an emotionally mature person.

5. **Immersion** – A person who is able to set aside their ego because they truly want to get to know another person and are committed to supporting each other emotionally. The immersion level is the final one and it is the extra step people take to commit to building a life together.

It is thought narcissists' emotional development is stopped somewhere in the third level when for whatever reason, they have trouble processing their emotions.

What Role Does Childhood Play in Becoming a Narcissist's Partner?

It is said that in romantic love, we choose a mate to help us resolve unresolved issues from our childhood. We are all conditioned and affected by our past experiences. That is a part of our uniqueness where no two people are exactly alike. The earliest experiences are the most impactful because babies or young people don't have the tools or filters to understand what they are experiencing. Children have no past perspective to be able to weigh against other similar experiences.

If an abusive parent has expectations of you and you don't fit their mold, you may be punished with a label. You can be "branded" with a nickname. This is a form of bullying. This causes damage and also causes the false perception by others that you deserve that label. Whatever is pinned on you is very difficult to shake because if it persists, you may begin to believe it, too.

The abusive parent can control you and others around you, in the way they talk to you or describe you to others. You can be mistreated in the same way a narcissist would treat a romantic partner with indifference and gaslighting. Being a dysfunctional parent's child may mean the boundaries between themselves and you are blurred. This is an abusive situation for a child because the parent doesn't think of the child as an individual, only as an extension of themselves. The parent may have unreal expectations of the child and this hurts the child's autonomy. When the child tries to separate from the parent in the normal healthy ways, the parent might lash out, because they have feelings of abandonment or are afraid of losing control. A narcissist has an uncanny talent for painting a negative word picture of a person they want to target. Their charm and confidence are so powerful; their children have no defense against their branding, gaslighting and other control tactics.

Breaking Generational Branding

Labels kept Jane away from Aunt Flo's daughters, the cousins she loved to spend time with when they were children. As an adult Jane's mother labeled Aunt Flo "selfish" and one of her daughters as "stuck-up", telling Jane her cousin looked down on her. It put a barrier to them having an adult relationship. All that stopped when at Aunt Flo's funeral, Jane talked to her cousin who told her that her own mother had done the same thing to her. They made a vow not to miss out on the rest of each other's lives. Powerful branding can be passed on from one generation to another. The seeds of dislike can grow in fertile soil without the people involved having an understanding of where this dislike is coming from, and without even knowing they are a victim of family branding.

JANE'S STORY: HOW PLAUSIBILITY IS USED IN GASLIGHTING

For years, ever since I can remember, my mother had been telling me I was difficult and strange. I could see the plausibility of why she would say that. A part of me suspected I was odd and a bit difficult, but what teenager doesn't?

There can be multiple contributing factors to why you can be lacking in self-esteem, and believing bad things about yourself, but the results are the same. And if you become a narcissist's partner, he will know exactly how to exploit those vulnerabilities.

SARA'S STORY: REMEMBERING THE MYSTERY DINNERS

Sunday nights meant dinner at my grandfather's house and Aunt Bea would cook a phenomenal dinner. Their house always smelled so good. You would think that would have been a good thing, but not for my mother.

On Sunday afternoon, as I was putting on my little patent leather shoes with the pretty lace trimmed socks, I would get my instructions. My mother told me; "Now be careful, Aunt Bea might put poison in the food". As I watched everyone gobble up her delicious food, me included, even at such a young age, I learned not to question my mother.

Every week it was the same thing and no one died, so Sara just stopped listening to what her mother was telling her. Sara learned not to question things that didn't made sense. She developed a compartmentalizing defense mechanism where she could put away those kinds of things so they would not bother her. It was her way of separating out things she was unable to deal with.

Narcissist's Partners: What qualities from Childhood Abuse Allows You to Stay in an Abusive Relationship?

* Not knowing yourself well enough, not in touch with your feelings.
* Lacking in self-esteem and feelings of low self-worth.
* Not knowing what you want.
* Being socially awkward.
* Misunderstanding of what you think is a healthy relationship.

- Drama has become normalized in your life and you find comfort in the familiar.
- Mistaking fighting for passion. We've all heard that myth about "make-up" sex, how much better it is supposed to be.
- Too much empathy, think you can change or heal your narcissist, because you see your self-worth in those types of behaviors.
- Too eager for validation, falls for the grooming and love bombing.
- Want to comfort them when they play victim, as you might have comforted a parent who lived for drama.
- Mistaking a narcissist's "take charge" attitude for stability.

CLARA'S STORY: FEELING "LESS THAN"

I tried so hard to please my mother. I remember when I was about 10, I had saved up from my small allowance to buy my mother a birthday gift. I walked the 4 blocks from my house to downtown and found in a small shop a lovely purse to replace her old worn-out one. I thought she would love it. When I gave her the purse on her birthday, she took one look at it, put it back in the box, and pronounced it too expensive. Then, we went back to the store, where she returned it, giving my money back to me. It was the worst feeling of rejection and not feeling good enough. That might be why as an adult, I love giving gifts, hoping to get it right.

When You Grow Up Feeling "Less Than" or Not Worthy of Love

When you grow up being told you are strange or difficult, you develop an internal negative script about who you are. Your self-esteem and feelings of self-worth suffer. Without basic confidence, you are left feeling less than and are susceptible to being taken advantage of by predatory people.

We all have an inner chatter going on in our heads about how we view ourselves. What we tell ourselves becomes wired into our brains. It is difficult to change that self-talk and that perception of who we think we are. A large part of healing those insecurities must start with intentional positive self-talk.

We know that many times in adulthood we act and react according to that inner script. For example: if you were told as a child, you were fat, you might carry that negative view of yourself into adulthood, even if you lost the weight, you still may be hypercritical of yourself.

The saddest thing is when a person doesn't feel worthy of love. Many women feel they have to be prettier, smarter, funnier, fill in the blanks, to be loved. This lack of self-esteem is one of the reasons people are willing to work harder in a relationship. This causes an imbalance in the relationship. It sets up a reinforcing cycle, where the person with the low self-esteem tries so hard to please their partner and if not reciprocated, they feel rebuffed and this further cements their perception of themselves as not being deserving of love. This cycle is like a self-fulfilling prophecy as you relive your childhood when you tried hard to please a parent and were not shown love in return. Everyone deserves to be loved unconditionally, so why do we feel we must jump through hoops to obtain it?

JANE'S STORY: THE RUNAWAY BOYFRIEND

I came home one afternoon to find my mother anxiously waiting to talk to me.

"You'll never guess who was just here!", she said,

"No, Mom, who?",

"Dave just left, he was looking for you", she said with a serious look.

"Oh, that's not like him", I thought, "He never just drops by"

Then her face turned grim, "He was very upset!"

"What was he upset about?"

She said: "He put his head in his hands and just kept saying", "I don't understand her, I can't figure out what she wants from me".

"Oh, that's not good", I said.

When I saw him the next day, he was very cool and re-fused to speak to me. Obviously, in hind-sight my mother must have told him a real "whopper" to put him off so badly. To this day, I don't know what she told him.

In Jane's story, you see her not even questioning Dave about what her mother said to him, or what he actually said. She had been so beaten down and conditioned just to take people at their word believing the worst about herself. She consoled herself by saying, *"It's ok, he's a senior, he was voted the most popular boy in his class, guess he didn't want me anyway."*

Healing from Childhood Abuse

Think of your childhood experiences in your family. Did you feel heard and understood, or were you expected to fit into a mold and go along? Were you praised for your uniqueness or scolded for being different?

If you were taught your worth depended on how others saw you, then how could you find out who you were? It is no wonder you found yourself trying to please people or heal them because that's where you were expected to find your self-worth.

Taking ownership of your feelings means you must be in a safe space to feel. If you have felt you had to hide your unique self, you will always feel "less than". This may make you think you are unworthy of love. You heal when you can accept yourself, know you are good enough and that you always have been. You heal by moving on in your life, not dwelling in past hurts, living an authentic life, not settling for less than you know you deserve.

If you relate to any of these stories or topics about childhood abuse, then this can help you get in touch with your own feelings to be able to heal your "inner child". You heal your inner child by embracing her, allowing her to be heard with no judgement, giving her a safe space to work on your unresolved childhood injuries. That's why if you are working on recovering from narcissistic abuse, you want to be kind, patient and generous to yourself.

TAKEAWAYS

- If you suffered abuse as a child, you must now reverse that abuse by becoming the nurturing "parent" to your "inner child".
- Having an understanding of the impact on an adult from an abusive childhood can help you heal.
- Knowing that childhood experiences can condition you to lose self-esteem and feel "less than" will give insight into why you may have stayed in an abusive relationship and help you to not be in one in the future.
- Know that you have always been worthy of so much more love and support than you may have experienced.
- Generational abuse and trauma bonds can be broken by gaining knowledge, the awareness of what has been happening, changing perceptions, and setting boundaries with positive actions for self-healing.

"I was always looking outside myself for strength and confidence, but it comes from within. It is there all the time." Anna Freud

CHAPTER TEN

Help, I am in a Toxic Relationship, What Do I Do Now?

SECTION I. DEALING WITH REALITY, EMPOWERING YOURSELF

Breaking the Trauma Bond

Narcissists are "dream weavers" and shape shifters, they get you first by reeling you in with all that love bombing and keeping you through the process of trauma bonding. It leaves you always wondering what is going on. Trauma bonding is best understood as what happens to you emotionally when you are in an abusive relationship. You get bonded to him by sharing a very high intensity relationship. Whether it is positive with high levels of romance and love making, or negative with abuse, this cycle of caring and then cruelty happening over and over, creates dependency on the narcissist.

That dependency is one of the main reasons abused women do not want to believe they are in that kind of situation and keep holding out hope for getting their relationship back on track. The trauma bond is so strong that even if you are not together anymore, that bond continues to pull you back in. The only way to not be pulled back in is to break that bond.

The day you wake up to realize you have been in an abusive relationship, you will know you must take steps to begin taking back your life. To see him clearly and throw off the invisible chains that have bound you to him, you must begin your journey to getting back to who you were. Don't be afraid of getting in touch with your feelings, to acknowledge them and say how you feel. If a person is not supportive of your feelings, you do not need that person in your life, no matter who they are.

It isn't easy to admit what has been happening to you, but setting boundaries for dealing with him is your path to finding closure. Sometimes the things you agonize over the most, are actually the simplest, but the most difficult to see.

You may have spent years wondering why you were so unhappy, or trying to figure out if the person you married still loves you. But, instead of wasting one more minute, you can break that bond by asking yourself one question and being prepared to answer it honestly:

"Would a person who really loves me, treat me that way?"

If you can step outside of your life for a moment, you will see the answer has to be no! You already know he is incapable of loving anyone other than himself, so how could he truly love you? You are the only one who can choose to break that bond with him. You are the one who can free yourself from the bond only you are feeling. You cannot expect anyone to rescue you. But you can rescue yourself by moving forward.

Blueprint for Moving Forward

- Pay attention to your feelings.
- Be honest with yourself about how his behavior makes you feel.

- Stop worrying about what he thinks.
- Stop worrying about what others think.
- Respect your feelings because whatever you are feeling is right and true.
- No one can tell you your feelings are unimportant or wrong.
- No one can tell you how to feel.
- If you feel disregarded, abused, or threatened, then you are being disregarded, abused, or threatened.
- Know you cannot change him. And he will not change.
- Do not listen to what he says, watch what he does.

One of the main reasons you've been feeling stuck is you have been listening to what he says. What he does will tell you who he is, not what he says. To counter all the damage that has been done, you will want to focus on healing yourself. You already know what a fragile ego he has, so taking him off the pedestal you put him on will not be as difficult as you thought. Just not paying attention to his demands will do a world of good for your self-esteem. You have spent all this time trying to please and appease him at your own expense. You have deprived yourself of love, while giving it willingly to him. Now it is your time to find love to give yourself.

Your Power

You will find your power when you reach deep to break the trauma bond by being honest with yourself. It is easy for you to lie to yourself or put off doing what you know you should do to avoid confronting the situation. By being brutally honest with yourself about how you empowered him, you can begin to empower yourself to move forward. Doing nothing is an action, and you may have chosen inaction more times than you realize.

You willingly gave him power over you. Taking ownership of your part in that abusive relationship will help to show you the way forward. He couldn't have treated you the way he did without your approval whether you knew that or not. Your love and caring empowered him. All this time, he has been using your energy. By staying, he felt approval from you. He saw it as a "green light".

If a man says to you in the beginning of a relationship; "I hope you can put up with me", you need to hear that for what it means. He is saying this because he has a track-record of abusing other women who eventually decided to not "put up" with him. Don't be guilty of thinking somehow you are different from the long line of broken-hearted women he has walked on or stepped over. You can't change him and he will not change for you. It is never about you. Thinking you are somehow different and can change a man is a waste of time, and heartache waiting to happen.

Every narcissist shows you who he is at some point in your relationship. How long you have been putting up with it is exactly how long you have refused to admit what you already know in your heart. It has been your choice all along. Coming to terms with this will free you to make better choices for your future.

You may have stayed with him for many different reasons. It could have come from being afraid of being alone or just being in a "honeymoon phase" fog, unwilling to see him for what he is. Some people stay because they don't want a person close to them to say "I told you so" or you just cannot envision life without him. It is hard to leave the familiar, no matter how bad, for an uncertain unknown. But, if you don't break this bond, it can break you.

Where do you go from here? The ball is in your court. He may or may not do something to make things better or free you. But, since it hasn't happened yet, there is a good chance as long as you are giving him the green light, things will never change. The trauma bond is strengthened the longer the abuse continues. You must take action to live in your power.

Instead of dreaming he might turn back into the prince you thought he was, you will have to become the strongest princess you can imagine. He will never be the person you thought he was; underneath all that charm you know he is the dragon. You must fight for yourself, be your own advocate, and rescue yourself from the jaws of that dragon!

The more you do for yourself, the more confidence you will have, as you widen your life beyond his control. Confidence is everything! With confidence, your self-esteem will blossom and you will embark on a positive path forward, taking yourself off the abuse merry-go-round. It is better if you don't do this alone. If possible, you want to find a solid support system of people you can rely on. All the strength you need to free yourself has always been right there inside you, but it is always a good thing to have supportive people around you. You will be able to witness how very strong you are by meeting challenges on your journey away from abuse.

We will be looking at a series of suggested actions, which will give you the tools to get to your goals. Of course, everyone's journey will be different depending on their situations and the cast of characters in their lives. These tools are not complicated and can be used by anyone to get into a better, healthier life.

It is no small task what has to be done to disentangle yourself from a regular relationship that is not working. To get out of a relationship with a narcissist can be much harder. But you may be pleasantly surprised. Where you thought things might be difficult, once you start standing up for yourself the relationship dynamics will change, sometimes drastically. This may open up new avenues for you to achieve your goals. You will appear to be a different person to him because he has known you to be compliant. Once you stop complying with him, his reactions may surprise you. He will be surprised too, to experience the "new" you.

Once you begin to stand up for yourself, he will look at you differently. Just as it has been a journey for you to come to realize who he really is, it might take him a while to see who you are now, with your new resolve.

Since you cannot change him, you will be changing yourself to change your situation and he will not like that. Narcissists don't deal well with change because they don't have your resilience. Another power you can call on is your ability to come back even stronger. People without mental health problems are able to bounce back from adversity. Challenges, well met bring to light strengths you didn't realize you had.

JANE'S STORY: THE BOX OF SUSHI

Jane was asserting herself after years of going along with everything Alex wanted. She had finally gone back to school. She began to get physically fit, by running and doing Japanese karate where she made new friends. She began to study the Japanese language, too. Immersing herself in a different culture gave her a way of distracting herself from her life at home. Jane enjoyed taking her kids to a local sushi bar, where the sushi man would put the live lobsters on the counter to dance. It was so liberating to have new interests of her own after so many years of supporting his interests.

Alex was very skeptical of the "new" Jane and decided to hate everything Japanese because Jane was finding so much pleasure in it. He was beginning to realize this was not just a phase she was going through, and saw life was changing.

One day, one of Jane's high school students wanted her to meet some relatives who had just arrived from Japan. The student suggested Jane and her family go together with her relatives to the local sushi bar. The relatives wanted to meet real American people. Jane was excited to try and speak to them with some of the beginning Japanese she was learning.

When Jane told Alex the dinner plans, he sulked. That evening the student came to Jane's house with her two uncles. The men were very kind and polite. They came into the house to invite Alex to the dinner, but he refused to go. He made an excuse about not feeling well, so off they went minus Alex.

As is the Japanese way, the uncles wanted everyone to feel taken care of and enjoy their meal. They hosted the dinner and insisted on ordering a large assortment of sushi to take-out for Alex. Jane tried to explain to them that Alex didn't like Japanese food, but this was beyond their comprehension. Jane was sure they had never heard of anyone who didn't like sushi. They also would have felt it impolite to exclude him, even though he had excluded himself.

When they arrived back to Jane's house, the uncles went right into the house calling Alex's name. In Japan, people go out of their way to show hospitality.

By then, Alex had already gone to bed. Before Jane could catch up with them and their large box of sushi, the uncles had gone into the main bedroom. Alex was already in bed when they opened the door and put the box on the dresser, trying to tell him the sushi was made especially for him.

They thought he'd be pleased to get such an impressive gift. Instead of being gracious, Alex got angry, jumped out of bed, and chased them around the house, holding the big box of sushi. His attempt to give back the sushi was not misunderstood, as the uncles exited the house as quickly as possible.

While this may seem like a funny story, to see a grown man in his underwear running around a house with a large box of sushi yelling at strangers, it was actually sad. It was sad because Alex didn't know what to do, he was frustrated about losing control over Jane and retaliated by disliking everything Japanese.

This story illustrates how narcissists become unnerved and unhappy about you asserting yourself and finding new interests. No matter how many years you have supported his pursuits, he will not be happy to do the same for you.

Some reactions you may encounter to the new you:

- He may try to love bomb you to convince you to go back to the way things were. Now you know that tactic, so you won't fall for it again.
- He may have such a negative reaction to you advocating for yourself, he may let the fire-breathing dragon out. That is when you must put your safety first.
- He may decide to get or already have a new supply and leave you.
- Once he realizes he cannot control you, he will work on controlling what is said about you to ensure he looks good.

"We cannot direct the wind, but we can adjust the sails." Dolly Parton

SECTION II. WHAT DO I DO NOW? PREPARING YOURSELF FOR THE NEXT PHASE, TAKING BACK YOUR LIFE

By the time you have decided to stand your ground and not allow yourself to be abused, you have probably been in a toxic relationship for a while, maybe years. This puts you at a disadvantage because you have been beaten down emotionally. You may overlook whatever form of abuse you have endured because it has become part of your daily life. That's what narcissists do; they normalize even the worst behavior by repetition. Human beings have the facility to adapt to anything. Just like in the story of the "boiling frog"; he doesn't jump out of the pot, not realizing he is being boiled, if the water is heated up gradually enough. The frog keeps adapting until it is too late. For you to break free will take work. It may take work in many different areas. This will be your journey of rediscovering you.

Pay attention to all sides of you. Nourish yourself! You are a multi-faceted person who needs stimulation from many different types of activities. When you dedicate your life to only serving the needs of a soul-crushing insatiably needy narcissistic partner, you stop meeting your own needs and shut yourself off from all those avenues which feed your sense of well-being. Here are some of the needs you may have neglected for him: Emotional, spiritual, intellectual, physical, friendships, sense of community, and many more you will find as you examine what support you would like to bring back into your life.

You have the ability to heal yourself and bring back your self-esteem by paying attention to what matters to you most. Start by doing things that nurture your spirit and give you joy. Spend time with friends, family and educational or interest groups you might enjoy. Rebuild support systems so you don't feel isolated and alone.

A Tool for Getting to Know Yourself Again
MAKE A LIST OF YOUR WANTS AND MUST HAVES TO BE HAPPY

Of course no one can be happy all the time, but by being aware of your happiness, you are taking a look at how mentally healthy you are. Do you feel optimistic about your life, do you see a bright future? People living a fulfilling, authentic life generally feel happy and satisfied with the direction of their lives.

To assess where you are, to begin to change your life for the better, write down your thoughts to help bring clarity to what is happening. Seeing things written down in black and white helps to clear away the cobwebs. Comparing where you are now to where you'd like to be on paper helps you to see why you have been feeling so crushed while simultaneously pointing you in the best direction. Being with a narcissist can take away your sense-of-self, even make you feel you have no life beyond the drudgery of serving his needs. Be brutally honest with yourself when answering these questions. This little exercise can help you get in touch with how you are truly feeling. Write down your answers to the following questions:

- Are you happy?
- If no, why do you think you are not happy?
- What do you need in your life to be happy?
- What changes could be made in your life to make you happy?
- What do you need in this relationship to be happy?
- What actions can you take to make yourself happier?

DECISION-MAKING EXERCISE

Make this deciding chart to bring clarity to difficult decisions. Here is another pen and paper exercise which can be effective in many different situations. It is useful when making difficult life changing decisions.

1. Take one sheet of paper (you may need more than one) draw a horizontal line near the top of the paper, for the heading.
2. Draw a vertical line down the middle of the paper, dividing it into two equal columns.
3. Put a plus, (+) sign at the top of one column, and a minus, (-) sign above the second column.
4. Now you have your decision-making tool. It's only one piece of paper, but if you are honest with yourself, writing down the pros and cons of your situation, you will be making a valuable roadmap for yourself.

For example: ask yourself, "What will I gain by leaving this relationship?" (list those answers in the plus column). Then ask yourself, "What do I have to lose by leaving this relationship?" Put that into the minus column. After you have recorded all your answers, see what they are telling you. I did that when leaving a place I loved. I was surprised to find my reasons for going, and why I needed to go, far outweighed the reasons to stay. Having this very simple, yet concrete way of clarifying your feelings can be a good source of strength and powerful tool for you. It allows you to be able to separate wants from must haves. It may also give you a new perspective on what you have been afraid to admit to yourself.

How to Slay the Dragon
STRATEGY # 1. NEUTRALIZING THE NARCISSIST'S POWER BY STANDING UP FOR YOURSELF

Relationships with narcissists are based on power imbalance. If you are unhappy, it is because he has most of the power, leaving you feeling irrelevant and unimportant in the relationship. One of the best ways to deal with that imbalance is to stand up for yourself. Do not accept his rules or his attempts at pulling the wool over your eyes or gaslighting you.

Because narcissists are all show, when challenged, their behavior is predictable. If you know ahead of time what to watch for, you will see the façade of this "superior being" begin to crumble. You may see how the image you built up in your mind is not his true self.

Take back your power by challenging his bad behavior. When challenged the narcissist will not know how to react. He has spent most of his life avoiding being challenged. This may even be a new thing for him. You may see a "deer in the headlights" reaction.

Narcissistic men can be misogynists. They think of their partners at best as little girls, who need their guidance, at worst as lesser beings. They are authoritarians, using tactics to keep you loyal and always ready to do their bidding. Knowing how important it is to them to keep that façade of superiority, you will see it doesn't take much to throw them off balance. You can stand up to him without arguing, without an emotional exchange, just by defying them with this one word, "no".

JANE'S STORY: STANDING UP TO HIM IN AN AIRPORT

Jane and her husband were walking through an airport with their daughter. Around that same time Jane had begun to realize her husband's actions were making her miserable and she needed to do something about it. She had already made up her mind she was not going to let him order her around anymore. They were having a disagreement about something, and he told her to pick up her daughter's suit-case. Instead of continuing their argument and giving him energy by fighting with him, she just walked on, without saying a word, and without the suitcase. He didn't know what to do. He was dumbfounded, he wasn't used to her not doing what she was told. Instead of the dragon coming out, his "go-to" meltdown, because they were in public he was unable to do much. He just stood there, mouth open. Jane continued to walk on with their daughter and he was left to carry the suitcase himself.

Doing that one simple thing was a giant act of rebellion for Jane. After all those years of being non-confrontational and just going along with his demands, she had finally done something to start her journey out of abuse.

Setting boundaries of what you will and won't accept is hard and can be daunting. But, just one small act of defiance like that can show you how to begin. You have already taken the first step when you de-cided to live in reality and get in touch with your own emotions.

STRATEGY # 2. NEUTRALIZING THE NARCISSIST'S POWER OVER YOU BY THINKING OF HIM AS A "BALLOON"

One way to conquer your fear of challenging your narcissistic partner is by visualizing him as an overblown balloon or any other puffed-up character. This can help you take your first steps when working on taking back your power.

Three ways a narcissist might implode when you challenge them by pushing back:

1. **Pop** – Fly into a rage.
2. **Fly Away** – Like when the air is let out of a balloon, not being able to deal with the situation, so they run away or hide.
3. **Deflate** – into miserable small people who are not in touch with the reality of who they really are. They might melt like a snowman in the sun because they are only playing a part of being the person they want you to see.

You will get a better understanding of who they really are by seeing their reactions. Just like in the children's fairytale, "The Emperor's New Clothes", no one wants to admit the emperor is less than perfect because he is "The Emperor", even though he is not wearing clothes. He might represent the narcissistic "balloon person" who is so puffed up, that everyone is afraid to tell him the truth. In the story, no one will admit reality until a small child yells it out. The narcissist will keep up his deception until someone challenges that perception. When he is challenged, he may become afraid of his false image slipping, and the fire-breathing dragon can appear to deflect any perceived threat.

STRATEGY #3. NEUTRALIZING THE NARCISSIST'S POWER OVER YOU BY NOT BEING FOOLED BY FALSE PROMISES
Jane's Story: How Alex's Rage Got the Best of Him

By now, Jane sees her life with Alex clearly. She has finally gotten to the point she knows they must separate and that's what she tells him. After years of Jane begging him to go to a marriage counselor, he gets scared realizing she is serious and takes her to two counselors. Both women tell Jane she should stay with Alex. One tells her in their city the ratio of women to men is 7 to 1, so she should stay with him. And they also tell her, as she approaches 40, it will be very hard to find someone new.

Alex is very contrite and promises to change, but his history tells Jane he won't. Deep down she knows he is incapable of change. He is so insistent and seems so willing to try, she gives him one last chance.

One night he is loading the dishwasher, showing her, he can do something to help. Jane questions him on one small thing, he snaps and out comes the dragon. He is in a rage. This time is different, she is prepared for it. She doesn't cower, or run away, she is not afraid of him anymore. She just stands there not adding fuel to his fire.

For the first time in their relationship, she dares to look him in the eyes, while he is in full dragon mode. What she finds is shocking, a person she has never seen before. His eyes look like lumps of coal, fully dilated from the adrenaline coursing through his body. This time his rage has gotten the best of him; his heart is racing, pumping blood furiously out to his body which is in "flight or fight" mode. In that very scary moment, instead of his heart recovering slowly, he is somewhere between wanting to kill her and knowing he can't do that. His brain slams on the breaks and he faints at her feet. It only takes a minute, but seems like much longer. While he is on the floor, she steps over him to get out of the small room he had shoved her into, she walks to the far end of an adjoining room to put distance between them. She had spent almost half her life witnessing his "meltdowns". As he comes to, he finally has to face how out of control he had been and it scares him, too.

That is what not being fooled by false promises and slaying the dragon can look like. Jane had become confident in herself and did not react to him. This allowed him to implode on his own. Just by treating him like you would anyone else, not weighing every word you say, not walking on egg shells, can move your life forward. It happens on its own when you decide not to comply with his wishes and not to be taken in by him. He cannot rely on you fixing things for him, he has to start taking some responsibility for his own actions. His acting out is not on you anymore. He cannot blame you for his bad behavior. You are on the road to neutralizing his hold over you and reducing his power of control.

TAKEAWAYS

- Dealing with the reality of your relationship empowers you to take action.
- You are able to rescue yourself when you break the trauma bond by saying no to him and meaning it.
- Moving forward and finding your inner power boosts your self-esteem and gives you confidence.
- Acknowledging your own feelings and worth allows you to stop abuse, because you understand no one can tell you how to feel or control you, without your permission.
- You can take back your power by standing up for yourself.
- Challenging his behavior changes the power dynamic by shifting it away from being all about him.

"If a problem has a solution, we must work to find it, if it doesn't, we must not waste time thinking about it." Dalai Lama

CHAPTER ELEVEN

Surviving the Break-Up Process

SECTION I. TAKING BACK YOUR LIFE AND MOVING ON

How to Know You need to Get Out and When

To paraphrase the Dalai Lama, if there is no solution, we must not waste time trying to solve an unsolvable problem. When you are clear that there is no way to salvage your relationship and realize staying in such a toxic relationship will certainly cause more harm to you and possibly others, then you know you must leave,

Leaving is never easy, but now with leaving in mind, you will want to prioritize your safety and peace of mind. To heal, you will need to forgive yourself for staying as long as you did. In your defense, it is nearly impossible to see a narcissist for who they are at the very beginning and later you tried to smooth things over. That is what we women do, we are the peacekeepers, but some things cannot be fixed. How could you ever imagine a mind like that? You are good, kind, caring and loving, not twisted, broken, devious and selfish.

You have given your all to make that relationship work. If you are lucky, your husband/boyfriend might have found someone new. It won't feel like you are lucky while going through it. It will feel devastating, a gut punch when you find out about her. But when you look back at that time, later in life, you will realize how fortunate you were to be able to get out relatively easily, as he will be the one who wants out.

If he goes off the rails, unleashing the dragon, as you start changing and making your own choices, that may help him to recognize his own dangerous behavior. I don't believe all narcissists intend to act badly; they just can't help themselves. Remember all personality disorders are on a spectrum and not all people with NPD are expressing all the traits. Some narcissists are more aware of their behavior than others.

Getting out of a relationship is a process, and just like you've gained clarity about who he truly is, you will gain clarity to know what to do. Knowing when to leave will be up to how you are feeling and what makes the most sense according to your situation and what is happening in the relationship. It may also depend on many other things that are going on in your life, so you may need to be patient. But if there is physical violence you must get help and get out immediately. Safety must always come first!

By using the deciding chart with the plus and minus columns from the last chapter, you will be able to see what is best for you. It may also shed some light on what your heart wants you to do. Be smart about protecting yourself, but remember it was your heart that got you into this relationship in the first place. Sometimes the heart must be temporarily overridden, so that you can move forward successfully. Leaving is never easy, but with your new confidence, you can do it!

When Anger is Good - Echoing

Are you angry? Are you coming to this point of deciding to leave with a lot of anger? This is normal. He has made you feel confused and helpless, maybe even hopeless, putting you down, possibly cheating on you. Now your anger is bubbling up, wanting to take your power back. For so long, you have worked so hard to push your anger down to keep the peace, but it is now wanting to come out.

When you have been on the receiving end of his anger, his put downs, and the dragon's rages, you may be so angry, you may be asking yourself, "Am I a narcissist?" The answer is, "no". You may start to feel you are acting like him, hurt and angry all the time. But, making you angry is just another tactic he is using to keep you feeding the dragon. Many women think about using his tactics on him.

Because narcissist's abuse cycle is predictable, this phase has a name. This is something that is present in many relationships like yours. It is actually part of the progression of your relationship and shows you are now coming out of the love bombing fog, and are aware of what he has been doing to you, through the devaluing and discarding stages.

When you begin to act like him, it is called "Echoing". Your anger and wanting to use his tactics on him are healthy for you to be feeling, but not to do. If you use his tactics on him, you risk becoming like him and you will end up not liking yourself very much.

If you are screaming at him, he feels powerful. If he is provoking you making you feel out of control, that makes him feel even more in control. Do not show him your anger. You are satisfying him by showing him he can make you upset. By not showing anger, you are not giving him energy. This will help to break his hold over you.

You haven't become a narcissist, but you have begun to fight back. That's a good thing. This is when anger can be good. It is good because it is your anger. Now is your chance to do something for yourself. Anger, like any other emotion you have given him, keeps him going, so you must shut it off. But, in a new way. Don't shove it down inside you, because that will only perpetuate your pain. Turn that anger into energy, and resolve to work on getting yourself out of this relationship. Your anger is good when used as energy, an impetus to stick up for yourself. This is when you have to turn his actions back on him and be indifferent to him. That does not make you a narcissist, it makes you a person who is now standing up and fighting back, the opposite of being a victim. You are forging your path to a new life.

How to Get Out of a Narcissistic Relationship

Things you can do to lower the temperature and not provoke further confrontations:

- Do not argue! You will never win since he must always be right, so it is pointless to argue with him.
- Whatever you want him to do must seem like it is his idea.
- Ignore his insults, he is only trying to get a reaction from you by trying to start an argument. He provokes you to get a reaction to use your reaction as a distraction from his actions.
- If you don't engage, there cannot be a fight.
- If you don't fight with him, he will not be getting any supply from you.
- Act as neutral and unemotional with him as possible.

If you leave him, you are reinforcing his story that he is the victim. If your situation does not allow you to leave immediately, here are some ways to prepare for that huge change. You will want to set boundaries on the relationship and build back your self-confidence by making changes in your life. You may need to build up your strength to take the inevitable next step. Build strength in any area you feel needs it. Planning activities by yourself or with friends will take your mind off of your situation and help find your way back to yourself. You want to build yourself back up, emotionally, mentally and physically. There are many things you can do as you start to take back your life to protect your heart and self-esteem from further damage.

It begins with setting boundaries and finding activities for yourself that are positive, uplifting and let you live in the moment. When you are about to leave, there are a myriad of feelings swirling around. You are in pain and you may feel guilty having been "gaslighted" into believing this break-up was all your fault.

Boundaries for Separating

Make sure to have a clear and unemotional conversation with him about how you feel and how you want to end the relationship, if he hasn't done that already. Make sure he understands completely what you are saying. Boundaries may be set for how you will communicate in the future. And if you feel you cannot communicate with him peacefully, you may want to limit your contact with him.

Boundaries will be different for different stages of your separation. A hallmark of a good healthy relationship is where a couple grows closer in intimacy and love. You are not used to consciously setting boundaries in a romantic situation. But, here, in a narcissistic relationship, they are the most important things you can do for your protection. Your narcissist partner was able to continue his abuse because you didn't define boundaries or he chose to ignore your boundaries. Either way, being with a person who takes you for granted and doesn't honor your values is demeaning, abusive and uncomfortable.

Don't be afraid to set boundaries, because you already know how. You set boundaries all the time, especially dealing with the unknown. Your phone tells you who is calling and if you don't want to talk, you don't answer. You lock your door, as a barrier to unwanted people coming in. You put in a code on your phone, to protect from having your information stolen. Knowing this, why wouldn't you set boundaries on an uncaring person who wants to keep you to continue to use you?

SETTING AND KEEPING BOUNDARIES:
- Setting boundaries is the most effective way to stop abuse.
- You will set boundaries according to what you need to feel safe from any form of abuse. Abuse doesn't have to be physical. In fact, many people believe that emotional and psychological abuse is much worse. Broken bones heal, but the trauma of emotional and psychological abuse can last a lifetime.
- Always avoid "power struggles" with him. That is "catnip" to the dragon. Remain calm and confident when you are

talking with him. Do not allow him to continue manipulating you emotionally. Walk away if he is disrespectful or tries to argue with you.

- Set boundaries to limit the time you spend with him. The less time spent with him, the less chance he has to try to draw you back in or use one of his tactics.

- By setting boundaries you rediscover your strength. You are proving your strength by standing up for your values and not wavering.

- Set boundaries by deciding what behaviors from him are acceptable and unacceptable. (Ex: Will you talk face to face, or only by phone?) Do not accept more empty promises and his changes in behavior toward you must be immediate.

- Setting boundaries is the same as making rules for how he must treat you.

- Boundaries do not have to be mutually agreed upon, especially with abuse. It is your right to set boundaries for your own safety and peace of mind.

- Only set boundaries you are able to keep.

- Make sure boundaries you set are ones that don't cause you more harm.

- You do not need anyone else's permission to set boundaries.

- If you don't set boundaries, then you are allowing the abuse to continue.

- Setting boundaries avoids conflict.

- Healthy boundaries will give you space to create a new life.

- People who don't respect your boundaries are the same people who took advantage of your lack of boundaries.

Setting boundaries will help you gain back the confidence you have lost. You are proving to yourself that you are able to protect yourself. What boundaries would you want to set? He's been setting the rules for you, probably for a long time. Now it's your turn.

"The time of greatest gain in terms of wisdom and inner strength is often that of the greatest difficulty." - Dalai Lama

SECTION II. HOW TO MOVE ON

You have already recognized the signs that your partner is a narcissist and you acknowledged that your relationship is unhealthy. Now you are preparing to get out of this relationship and move on. You are setting boundaries about how you and he are going to interact with each other aiming to take as much emotion out of it as possible. This can be a very emotionally challenging time for you. Here are some suggested steps to take to make this process as easy and stress free as possible:

Prepare emotionally. Be aware that you may be experiencing a variety of different emotions. You might be grieving the death of the relationship you thought you had or afraid to be on your own. You may even feel relief, when you realize you will be set free from the abuse. You will need time to process all that you have been through and deal with all the emotions you are feeling.

Find support from people who know you. That may be from family or friends because they know you best and want to see you come out of this well. They can offer you the love you will need at this time. If you are completely alone, self-love can go a long way to helping you through this process. You must be patient and kind to yourself.

Get support from professionals. If you feel you will need professional help seek out a good family mental health professional. You may also want to consult with a lawyer, who can tell you your legal rights and give you advice in other areas. A good female lawyer, after hearing why you are leaving that relationship will inquire about your safety before she proceeds further.

Make a safety plan. If you are worried about your safety, you will want to find a safe place to stay. Talk to friends and relatives. If there is physical abuse or you feel unsafe consider how you might protect yourself.

Make an exit plan. That might include deciding on when you are leaving and where you are going. If you are going to a new city, you might want to try to secure a job first. If you can work from home that is helpful, or if you are working at a big company or the government, you might be able to transfer to a new place. Depending on how bad your situation is with your partner, you might want to put some distance between you and him. You may also need to separate your finances. This would be a good time to get that pen and paper out and look at your needs, wants, and must haves.

Keep track of any physical abuse. Document each incident with a date, place and narrative. This could be important information for later if you think you might need it to build a legal case.

Always be aware of your mental health. Check in with yourself often. It is ok to go through different stages of grief and feelings of uncertainty as long as you are feeling safe. That should all resolve. it just takes different amounts of time for different people. And some people may want to work with a mental health professional to help them resolve those feelings. Make sure to support yourself by doing things that bring you joy.

Things You Can Do for Yourself

When changing your life, you have a choice to change your focus. If you continue to look backwards, you can never move forward. Choose to focus on your future!

You will find distractions are very welcome during this emotionally fueled time. Here are some suggested activities to help you unwind and take your focus off your messy situation, so it has time to play out naturally. Do things for yourself with an eye for what you want your future to look like.

Here are some things you might try: Walk in nature; travel to make new friends and find out new things about yourself; join clubs; join a gym to work on yourself and get physically fit (always a plus for self-esteem and great revenge, when you look good). If you can't afford a gym, walk or run with a friend or visit botanical gardens, or do something else to enhance your health. You can learn a new language; it is free online with the Duolingo app. Then maybe later you can visit the country where that language is spoken and enjoy using what you have learned. Take control of your finances, start with a major financial institution where they have free tutorials online, or a financial planner, or adult classes. Get a makeover, available in beauty and department stores for free. Get a new hair style or change your hair color. There are endless ways you can lift yourself up and choose to focus on moving forward and being positive.

Reconnect with old friends and use this time for spending with family. You may not want to be around people you love so as not to share the misery you are feeling, but give them a chance to help you. Let them know how grateful you are to have them. Get a membership at a massage spa, or volunteer at an animal shelter, homeless shelter, or museum. If you can spend time helping others, it is always a boost for your soul.

Look at this big change in your life as an opportunity to go in a new direction mindful that a new beginning gives you a gift. It is a second chance for you to show up for you. A space for growth allows you to do the things you always wanted to do. Meet the moment with intention rather than seeing it as a defeat. It can be the time for immense growth and opportunity.

How to Deal with the Awkward Times

If you are still living together, and your narcissist can't make up his mind as to what he wants, it will be a challenge to know how to deal with this situation. You have had the talk about ending the relationship, but you are still working out details. You have set boundaries, so you will not be involved in his manipulation and are still trying to be civil to each other. What do you do during this time of indecision? This is where friends can play a very important role.

This story shows how opportunities for happiness exist among what you thought were the "ruins" of your life.

MARY'S STORY: THE BACHELOR AUCTION

Mary tells her story: I had never heard of a Bachelor Auction before and rather than waiting for my mostly absent husband, to come home, I decided to take my friend, Cynthia up on her offer. She had taken pity on me and dragged me out for an evening. It was an amazing event, very glitzy and glamorous.

The bachelors ranged in age from 26 to 53 and were some of the most handsome, eligible bachelors in that city! At the time, I was 48 and not feeling so good about my life or myself, so this was a wonderful distraction from my sad situation. The first event was a "Meet the Bachelors" reception. Cynthia and I had one hour to walk around and meet them.

As if the champagne were not enough, the bachelors were dressed in tuxedos, and their date packages, (that's what they called the date they had planned) were fantastic. One "dream date" was outlined in the catalogue as: "Imagine a date with a super handsome man, he picks you up in a limo, whisks you off in a private jet to an island, horseback riding on the beach, then a swim together, join him for a couple's massage at a 5-star hotel, afterwards you'll change into a beautiful gown to have a meal cooked by a Michelin star chef and dance the night away under the stars." It was like being on a TV show, only all you had to do was come up with a few thousand dollars, for charity and you could go on the date of your choosing.

As I walked around looking to talk with a few bachelors, I recognized one from the bachelor catalogue who caught my eye. He was so friendly and fun to talk with. He told me what he did for a living and how he had come up with all the different parts of the date he was offering.

The auction itself was so much fun, but Cynthia and I did not bid.

Two days later, in the late afternoon, my phone rang. The voice on the other end said, "Hi, I'm Jim, remember talking to me at the Bachelor Auction?" I couldn't believe it; he was the person I had enjoyed talking with the most. So much so, I had said to Cynthia, "I wish I could bid on Jim, because he was so nice". "That Cynthia, she must have given Jim my number". I was amazed that he was calling me.

When Jim told me a friend had just given him two tickets to the theater, I decided to say yes, I would go. Then another amazing phone call only a few minutes later, my husband called to tell me he planned to come home that night. I had to tell him this time I was the one who was going out.

And that was the beginning of a friendship that got me through my last month before I left to start my new life. As it turned out, Jim and I went out a few more times for beautiful dinners and a "bachelor auction worthy" picnic on the beach. Jim turned out to be an important part of my support group, by being there for me during a very bad and draining time. Friends made a world of difference.

Now, I know what you might be thinking. I have talked at length about "no such thing as a "Prince on a white horse" coming to rescue you." In this story, especially the way it worked out seemed like a dream come true, but Jim was in no way a prince. He was however, a very positive force that was there for Mary right when she needed and appreciated the diversion. It is very difficult to "tough it out" alone when you are trying to detangle your life from a narcissist.

This story is for all those who say, how do I stop thinking of my ex, what do I do? It shows that when you choose to be open to opportunities, no matter what your age or situation and put yourself out there, you never know what good things the universe may send your way.

TAKEAWAYS

- When you cannot salvage your relationship and realize it is toxic, then you know you must leave.
- If you are being abused mentally and emotionally, you must set realistic, strong boundaries that you can live with.
- Leaving may be one of the most difficult things you will ever do, but can also be one of the most empowering.
- Find a way to get through this difficult time in the kindest way possible, for you and him.
- Fighting with him is giving him your energy. Cut off giving him energy by being as peaceful and unemotional as possible.
- Use your anger toward him for all he has done to you, for the energy you will need to get out gracefully.
- If there is ever physical abuse, you must leave immediately.
- The person who doesn't want to honor your boundaries is the same person who took advantage of you because you didn't have any before.
- Go into this with as much openness as possible for the positive opportunities that will come out of it.

"If you can't fly, then run, if you can't walk then crawl, but whatever you do you have to keep moving forward". Martin Luther King, Jr.

CHAPTER TWELVE

How to Recover to Get to Thriving

SECTION I. GETTING OVER HIM, WORKING ON CLOSURE

Finding Closure through Clear Thinking

Be honest with yourself. You thought your relationship was a love affair for the ages, or so he convinced you to think of it that way. If you now know it was not, you have realized he wasn't the person you thought he was. When you stopped carrying his part of the relationship, there was no relationship. How many people do you text or call, and if you stop texting or calling them, you never hear from them? If people stop showing up for you, it is not your fault.

It felt so real. Yes, that's what narcissists do. You deserve so much more. You will find closure when you can value yourself, your uniqueness and your feelings more than the dream you thought you had with him.

Who and what you give your time and energy to define who you are. Do not give your precious energy, your power to anyone who is not deserving of it. Love should not be based on what you have to offer. You should know you have a lot to offer. You want and deserve love with someone who loves you for yourself and nothing more. If you give your love in a relationship and it is not reciprocated, it breaks your soul.

You want to stay as far away as you can get from being around toxic people. This is important because you are trying to get out a situation that took a toll on your self-assurance and self-esteem. When you surround yourself with real friendships, people who are healthy and capable of appreciating you for yourself, you will find the love and happiness you deserve. But first take the time to appreciate you and give yourself gentle time to heal. An authentic loving relationship will bring understanding to how hollow your narcissistic relationship had been. This will help to bring closure.

Let's Flip It!

Congratulations to you, you've come so far! You are now able to spot narcissistic traits and tactics, you are on guard for the first signs of love bombing, and you know the game he's been playing. You now want to work on yourself to put this whole relationship/marriage in your rear-view mirror!

Here are some reverse-engineered tactics for you to use. They are designed to help you shut all the negativity down, both from him and what is going on in your own brain from love addiction withdrawal. These tactics are meant to be antidotes to the tactics he used to keep you being his supply. They can also help you get over him. Just as your anger can be a good thing because it fires you up to take action, flipping the script on him gives you tools to get to closure. That is your immediate goal, to shut down his control over you. Your ticket to the new you.

Your narcissist has controlled and manipulated you, by using some of these same tactics you will flip on him for your healing. They will not be used against him in the way he used them on you. They will be used for your peace of mind and can show you the power you may not think you have. These tactics are useful as a way to extricate yourself from the cycle of abuse and break the trauma bond.

Now in the process of liberating yourself, you don't want him or anyone else to have that kind of hold over you ever again. You know you need to cut all ties with him, but either he keeps reeling you back in, or your own brain is doing that for you. By not giving up on him yet, you are keeping yourself mentally and emotionally chained to him. This is habit, chemistry, addiction, all those things you will need to break free from in order to put this behind you, for good.

Taking back your power and moving on can be very difficult, if you continue to act the same way you did throughout the relationship. Your actions have worked to his advantage, this is why you will want to flip that script. Try to see your relationship from a different angle and use the abusive aspects to your advantage by reminding yourself how much you don't want to go back. It can help to set and keep boundaries for your healing.

You don't have to worry about turning into a narcissist because the way you will be using these tactics will not be the same way as he used them against you. You don't have to be mean or vindictive. When you realize you cannot change him, then you know your only choice is to change how you think about him, your reactions and how you act with him going forward.

Many women are "hoovered" by their exes, trying to suck them back into a relationship. If you remember this, you will see how it can happen. The narcissist's game is for you to think you need him, but in reality, he needs you much more than you need him. This makes sense, because if you leave you are losing abuse and misery, but for him he loses his supply, his life's breath. Without that adoration he is sunk. If you can look at it this way, you will see you actually have the upper hand.

Start with the **three main stages of the "Narcissist's Relationship Cycle",** but to flip the script you will be flipping the stages. You will take them out of their original order. Let's see how these tactics can help to bring back your personhood and free you.

Devaluation: You know how that feels, this is the phase he moved into after the honeymoon phase. Congratulations, again! You have already accomplished this tactic. The moment you realized who he was and what he was doing, you have already devalued him. His actions are not a mystery anymore. He may have already shown you his real self when revealing his mistress or letting the dragon out. You know he is not the man you thought he was. He has fallen off the pedestal and you will never idolize him again. Reminding yourself of how far you've come in your discovery of who he is will help you to stop questioning what he is doing. It will enable you to move on, and not go back.

Discarding and Leaving Him: Completely detaching from him might not be possible. You might still be living in the same house or share children with him. But there are things you can do to keep moving forward in this phase. You can get out of the house, as soon as possible, or best case, he leaves. You may need legal help to detach completely from him given all the ways you may be attached. But you can discard him in your mind. This is important because the whole allure of him may still be living in your mind. To counteract these thoughts you can remind yourself of who he truly is.

You can start giving yourself closure by moving on mentally and emotionally. Cut contact as much as you can. You have no obligation to give him anything. He almost made you lose your mind, so you don't have to worry about his. The more you can diminish the role he plays in your life, the faster you will be able to put him out of your life and out of your heart.

Idealization and Love Bombing: You can flip what he did to you by not idealizing him anymore. Elevate yourself. Put the same energy you used to make all his dreams come true into making your own dreams for a brighter future a reality. You will now become your own supply, as it should be, giving yourself permission to be healthy, happy, and having a life filled with joy. This is where the positive self-talk can make a big difference.

Indifference: Yes, indifference can be a great source of strength and tool for you when trying to heal yourself. He doesn't deserve anything from you, so you can work on being indifferent to him. He has been indifferent to your feelings, now you will use your indifference toward him as a shield to protect yourself from further abuse. You set boundaries, control how often there is contact, and don't share your feelings, good or bad, with him. The indifference you will cultivate can free you emotionally. You will be doing this for you, not to hurt him. He will cry foul, say he's in pain, he's the victim. The same person who dumps you to marry his mistress says he was hurt because he found out you married someone quickly after your divorce. If that is what he does, it is further proof of his narcissism.

Writing as a Tool for Getting in Touch with Yourself and Getting Over Pain

Writing helped me when I needed it, to get the pain out and onto the paper. When you write things down, those things serve as powerful reminders and warnings to never go down that road again. Such a small thing as a poem, if written from the heart can protect you. It is another way to gain clarity and to get the negative emotions out.

I wrote the following poem at the very end of a marriage, decades ago, before I ever thought of a narcissist. I am sharing this poem with all its raw emotions, to show you if you relate to this, you will know you are not alone. When you go through abusive experiences, they can be a jumping off point for positive change and healing. It can also be an impetus for creativity. I know it helped me.

I drew clear boundaries, gave him a date when I was planning to leave, if he didn't give up his girlfriend. In this marriage, for most of it, I never felt abused, sometimes puzzled, but was perfectly happy, because I had learned to make the best of what I had. But after I found out about his affair, every day was a new drama and I never knew who was coming home that evening.

Looking back, I know how lucky I was compared to so many women who are strung along for years. So, this poem is not about the man I married, but more about the man he became when his affair was revealed. He became angry because his secret was revealed.

The difficult part came from his ambivalence when he was not clear about what he wanted. The pain that it caused was most probably compounded due to his ability to keep me in the dark throughout the marriage. I lived under the illusion we were both so happy.

THE WORST TYPE OF MAN

Whenever woman get together, we trade war stories about the "users". How they hit and run, relentlessly take, while never giving back. I always thought they were the "Worst Type of Man"!

Now I know there is a far more dangerous breed, ones who act strong and committed, but are only committed to themselves! Not until you said the words, "I see no future with you", did I fully grasp the meaning of a new title, more than a "user", you are a "destroyer"!

You assaulted my senses on every front, lied to me, built up hopes and fostered dreams. You took the very best from me and turned it into dust. Using me up and wearing me down with your deceit and indifference!

Silence is a killer, it dehumanizes, saying more than words ever could. It sucks the very life out of a person, constant disapproval of her very existence. The weight it puts on the heart seems insurmountable. It draws you down so far till all you want is to become part of the earth.

The worst kind of man kicks her when she is down, when she's the most vulnerable. He accuses her of disloyalty in the middle of his betrayal. Uses erratic behavior to keep her off balance, lying, then flaunting his affair, wearing her down with petulance, then trying to grab forgiveness and absolution, falsely resurrecting hopes and dreams with feigned kindness in the middle of the kill!

The worst kind of man is not content with just the spoils, he has to see her bleed, holding her close to make sure she stays available to be slaughtered again and again!

Journaling

Journaling can be a powerfully positive tool for you to reflect on and gain clarity about your situation. It is a place to gather your thoughts, foster your personal growth, and seek refuge. If you are doing circle thinking, where your thoughts just go round and round in your head, writing them down in a consistent way will get your thoughts out, give insight, and peace of mind.

Journaling can take many forms. It doesn't have to be a physical journal. I write my thoughts into an email on my phone, send them to myself and file them together. But, putting pen to paper is thought to be more therapeutic. Do whatever suits your lifestyle. You would be surprised how many celebrities and CEO's journal. It can be for clarity, or gratitude to count your blessings, or for whatever you want it to be.

Write down your thoughts at least once a day. Fill it with positive thoughts for yourself, your aspirations, hopes and dreams. It can be your "cheerleader", if you list your best qualities and talk to yourself about how you can build on those strengths. You can also use it to keep track of your progress and celebrate little victories. Never underestimate the power of positive self-talk.

See what suggestions might resonate with you. Write down what things might help to give you the support you need. The suggestions are here to show you how important it is for you to show up for yourself by being proactive and planning uplifting activities.

If you didn't do this during the breaking up process, you might want to re-visit these suggestions, especially if you are moving to a new place where you don't know many people. Much of the pain and hardship of breaking up and healing comes from having to do it all on your own. The idea behind these suggestions is to help you to move forward in building a new healthier life. Stay as positive as you can, knowing you will attract what you believe you deserve. If you are secure in yourself, happy with your life, you will attract people who will see you that way, not someone who could become their supply.

"Life is not about waiting for the storm to pass. It's about learning to dance in the rain" Vivian Greene

SECTION II. STARTING OVER IS NOT EASY, WHAT RECOVERY LOOKS LIKE

Once you are separated, he may continue to try to make your life more difficult. He is frustrated he cannot control you and will find any means available to take revenge. He now sees you as an adversary who has taken away your affection. He may try to knock you off the pedestal he thinks you have put yourself on. Jane had two incidents where Alex played games with her. In the beginning, Jane did not want anything from Alex, except a very small child support check. She quickly gave even that up because dealing with him was never worth the aggrevation.

JANE'S STORY: THE GAME OF HIDE THE CHECK

Jane said, "The first month, the check was brought to her house in Alex's car, but Alex was not behind the wheel." Jane went out to the car. The person driving the car told her the check was somewhere in the car and it was her job to find it. He was kind enough to help her look. Eventually the check was found in the glove compartment.

JANE'S STORY: THE GAME BECOMES MORE PERSONAL

The next month, Alex drove over to give Jane the check in person. She went out to greet him. After a brief hello, Alex said, "Here's the check", handing it out the open car window. Even after the last month's game playing, she never expected what came next.

As Jane reached to take the check, Alex began to back the car, slowly down the driveway. Jane stopped; she couldn't believe he wanted to play such a childish game. It felt demeaning to have to run after a retreating car. She felt like she was a dog, chasing a bone. She continued to walk, thinking he would stop. She was giving him the benefit of the doubt, just like she had done so many times before. She tried one more time to reach for the check. Her mind didn't comprehend his actions, as she wondered to herself, "He couldn't really be doing this, could he?" But he continued backing up the car. She stopped, deciding not to fall for his game anymore. He drove away with the check still in his hand, showing out the open car window. Chalk that up for team Alex, that day!

These two stories show classic narcissistic, arrested development. Even in the midst of a sad divorce, a broken home, trying to do the best for the kids to build new lives, a narcissist has to try to get the best of the person who was once his supply. This game playing, one-upmanship would never stop, because he had to see her suffer to heal his bruised ego. And what really motivated him was, she didn't seem to be suffering. Over the years she learned there was no end to his immaturity or his wanting revenge. She was resolved to never allow him to have an effect on her life again.

Tips for Finding Your Happiness During Recovery

You will be able to find your happiness when you realize you do not care what your ex does. His life is now only relevant in terms of the children you may share. And in time, kids grow up and you do not have to coordinate anything with him. If his influence on your life is still too hurtful after the separation/divorce, you may want to think about putting physical distance between you and him. Some narcissists do not know how to let go. You cannot trust they will not try to make you look bad. Because you know you only have power over how you act. It doesn't hurt to be polite, but never show him any emotions, unless they are friendly, happy ones.

For your own recovery, put all your energy into finding yourself again. Being away from him will not end the drama both mentally and emotionally, unless you actively seek to end it and build yourself back up. Remember with the weight of an abusive and stress- filled relationship off you, you'll feel lighter and more resilient.

You control your life by the choices you make, every day. Stand up for what you believe, emphasize and value what is good. Don't let negative people bring you down. You need people in your life who will respect you and love you for who you are. Anyone who wants to change you doesn't deserve your time or energy. Don't worry if you get down sometimes, healing takes time and it is perfectly fine and natural to feel a variety of emotions. Just like breaking any habit, there can be backsliding, or "falling off the wagon", but your resolve to detach and discard him for all the trauma he caused you will keep you going.

Your emancipation does not sit well with the partner you are leaving. Beware of the "flying monkeys", his minions who will do their best to derail your efforts. He will start a smear campaign to control the narrative around your leaving. His supporters will then go out and spread the "gospel" according to him. He can love bomb all the people you know, to ensure they think well of him, to win them over. Even your family is not out of bounds for his surreptitious campaign to make him look like the victim. (I have seen this happen to a dear female friend of mine, as her family gave him more sympathy and support than they gave her.) Sadly, people take sides during a divorce and you may be labeled the "bad one". This campaign of lies about you can ruin your life, and many times you have no idea where this hate is coming from. Another "head-turner", the ability of a narcissist to get his hateful propaganda out and have it believed by so many people.

So, what can you do? You cannot let this derail your efforts to get to a healthier emotional space. Never apologize or feel guilty for what you need to do, or have done to put the abuse behind you and heal. Live in your power and your authenticity. It has taken you a long time and a lot of hard work to break free of the trauma bond you had with him. The flying monkeys may even tell you they are jealous of you because you have such a good life. They would rather have seen you crumble. Don't allow their pressure to get to you. Stay strong by thinking of all the people who are depending on you. Also, think of grandbabies and possibly great grandbabies that you will be able to help in the future as you get stronger every day gaining back your life. The future is waiting for you, don't disappoint your future self.

Give yourself as much time as you need to heal. Doing mindfulness practice like yoga or meditation can help you live in the present and will help you keep calm. Living in the present means you don't spend time thinking of the past. The past is gone, and the future is not here yet, so you can be happy right where you are. The people who are the most content with their lives report they are happy right where they are. If you spend time thinking about what you are grateful for in the present, it keeps your mind from wandering back to your perceived loss. I like the saying, "there is a reason the present is called that, because every day is a gift." A chance to start over! You can celebrate this new day by promising yourself to live in the moment and make the most of it. Living in the present allows you to stay engaged with your life, so you don't miss the good stuff.

Fight for yourself! You are worth it. If you are changing, and moving forward making your life better, there will be no time to think about him. Deciding what you want to include in your new life will help shape what you do and what it will look like. If you have an idea of where you want to go, there's a better chance you will get there.

Be thankful you are out of it and look at what you were able to accomplish, even if it was only to get out in one piece. Give yourself mental, emotional and physical hugs. Cherish every moment you can spend with friends and family. You are now free to choose how you will spend your time. The more time spent looking forward, rather than remembering past hurts, the faster you will heal. I have learned there is no way to predict where you will land, but for me it has always been right where I wanted to be. Having a good life is not always easy, but is always worth fighting for.

Dating After a Narcissistic Relationship

Many women want to jump right into dating to boost their self-esteem, to feel wanted and desired again. Do not feel you must adhere to any timeline. And never worry about your age. This is all part of being kind to yourself, doing things when you feel ready. You can do solo activities, make new friends, stay home with a good book, or a furry friend. Do whatever you feel like doing, because everyone heals in different ways, taking different amounts of time, doing different things to get to where they would like to be. Remember, you will not get back to where you were. You don't want to go backwards because those actions led you to the wrong relationship. You want to strive to continue moving forward, learning from past mistakes. Try to learn something new each day, if possible. You may find your life may not look anything like you envisioned, but that is ok. It is part of allowing yourself to find a new life, and being open to different experiences. When you are ready, you may find life will take you to a better place than you might have imagined. After you have gone through the "living hell' of being in love with a narcissist, you will be kinder, stronger, more empathetic with much more to give. You have been there and triumphed. People will notice. Your kindness and self-assurance will put you on a good path, for finding your joy!

MORE WAYS TO FIND HAPPINESS THROUGH BETTER EMOTIONAL HEALTH

Stop looking for external validation from other people's opinions. Conducting your life for other's opinions, will not bring you joy. If you don't like what you are seeing online, don't read it! Don't post it, unless you are ready for any kind of comment.

Know you are good enough and always have been. You will know you don't need praise from other people when you fully embrace your self-worth and know you have everything you need to live a good and happy life. In the end, it never will be anyone else's job to make you happy. Only you have the power to make yourself happy, by living an authentic life.

Make an effort to accept yourself. When you don't accept yourself with all your human flaws, then you are stopping yourself from finding happiness. You can never measure your life by anyone else's. You may think someone has a better life than you do, but if you knew what their life was like, you might be surprised to find yours may be better. It is not possible to find your happiness, if you are always trying to be like or better than someone else. Self-acceptance right where you are is one of the main keys to happiness.

Be aware of other people's boundaries. Focusing on only what you can control in your own life, allows you to make healthy connections while honoring the other person's autonomy. It also helps to limit disappointment.

Past is not prologue. What happened in the past doesn't have to dictate your future. You also have the choice in the way you think about your past. When looking at it as a learning experience, you can take from it what will help you build a better future. In fact, if past problems are weighing on your mind, you might "flip" that thought and realize you don't have to go through that again. You already have been there and know how to stay away from that unhappiness. Think of knowing the past as a type of inoculation, preventing you from catching the "unhappiness bug", again.

Find ways to contribute to your community. By helping others, you can find your own happiness. Helping others gives you another way to connect with people. It can give you a purpose and a sense of satisfaction and accomplishment.

> *"There are far, far better things ahead than any we leave behind." C.S. Lewis*

SECTION III. DON'T LOOK BACK, THRIVE

New Life, New Space

Looking at the cup half full is always better than looking at it half empty. It is easy during a break up to mourn the loss of the relationship for what you thought it was or could have been. You might find yourself wallowing in the waters of confusion and going through withdrawal from the lack of those love chemicals. By rehashing your old life in your mind, you are prolonging the time you are staying in that abuse, only this time you are doing it to yourself.

Every minute you spend questioning, looking back, thinking about the past or agonizing over the future, is a minute of your life you have lost. Try to look at the break up from a positive perspective. What are the positive things that are now happening and will continue to happen without the stress of abuse from a narcissistic relationship?

Without his control over you, monopolizing your time and energy, you will have the freedom to discover who you are again. You will have the space to welcome amazing people and opportunities to come into your life!

A Whole New World

I look back on my life, after divorce and heartache, and I see a vision of my life after that break-up. I had lost my self-assurance, my self-identity, and was told I was too old to ever find love again. But sometimes life is kind and this is what I found.

I found a person who was very positive. A person who loved me for myself, even though I spent every night of our first year together crying. My mind could not completely leave the toxic relationship I had already physically left. Somehow, he seemed to understand. He was a lot younger than me, and had a job which was his obsession. He was not exactly marriage material, but we made it work. We celebrated our 10th wedding anniversary in Scotland where he drove us all around the country, never tiring of me asking him to stop, every few feet to take photos of the gorgeous views. He showed me in so many thoughtful ways, how much he valued me. We were ecstatically happy, traveling together. We went to 9 countries in Asia, drove all over Europe, putting his little car on the train from England to France and back. He reminded me of my dad, always smiling and happy when he was pursuing the things he loved. I found happiness living without the drama. He was the furthest thing from a narcissist, never had the time for negativity or game playing. He was very secure in who he was. The universe gave me another chance at happiness. And it keeps giving, no matter what my relationship status is, because I am happy on my own, as well.

I want to thank you from my heart to yours for reading this book. I am hopeful it will give you much needed insight into this complex and thorny problem of narcissism, which has caused so much devastation in women's lives. It is my hope you will find in yourself all the strength, beauty and answers that you already possess.

Now, I find my joy in helping others to find their happiness. I would be most grateful and honored if you would share with me through the website, what information in the book was the most helpful to you. I've been told it has been very helpful to women who learned so much about what they wished they had known when they were younger, or women who said they never before understood a man's puzzling behavior and found the answers to their questions here. Remember it is your goodness that the narcissist takes advantage of, never anything you did wrong; no matter how much they try to put their faults on you. Because knowledge is power, I hope you now have the power to keep yourself safe, to not just survive, but thrive, and soar!

If you enjoyed this book, please put a review on Amazon and share it with friends, to let people know this resource it available for them, too.

Hoping to meet you at: http://www.theoppositeoflove.com

Wishing you a wonderful life filled with good health, love, laughter and joy!

TAKEAWAYS

- Being honest with yourself about your relationship will help you find closure.
- Flipping the narcissist's abuse cycle for your own use will give you ways of discarding him.
- Using tactics that were used on you doesn't make you a narcissist, if used in a different way to help you get over a love addiction.
- You will find happiness by taking proven steps toward becoming more emotionally healthy.
- By not allowing yourself to dwell on your old life, you will be better able to move on into your new life.
- Beware the "flying monkeys", who do his bidding by spreading lies about you, trying to derail your new life.
- If you do the work to free yourself, you will be making space for your new life to begin. Space for all the new wonderful opportunities to come.
- You may find your new life, better than you could have imagined it to be.

REFERENCES

American Psychological Association. *Manipulation*. APA dictionary of psychology. https://www.dictionary.apa.org/manipulation.

Arnold, C. 2010. *Understanding Schemes & Emotion in Early Childhood*. London: Sage Press.

Bailey, M.J. 2003. *The Man Who Would Be Queen*. Joseph Henry Press.

Bancroft, L. 2002. *Why Does He Do That? Inside the minds of angry and controlling men*. New York: Putnam and Sons.

Bandy, L. 2017. *Dangerous Case of Donald Trump: 27 psychologists and mental health experts assess the president*. New York: Martin Press

Braza, J. 2020. *Practicing Mindfulness*. North Clarendon, VT: Tuttle Publications.

Brown, N.W. 2001. *Children of the Self-Absorbed: A Grown-Ups Guide to Getting Over Narcissistic Parents*. Oakland, CA: New Harbinger Publications.

Crown, D.P. 2007. *Personality Theory*. Ontario, Canada: Oxford University Press.

Davis, S & Eppler-Wolff, N. 2009. *Raising Children Who Soar*. New York: Teacher's College Press.

Diem-Wille, G. 2011. *The Early Years of Life: Psychoanalytical Development*. London: Karnac Books Ltd.

Dr. Carter, Les. *How Narcissists Show their True Colors*, YouTube Video.

Dr. Carter, Les. *How Ugly Can Narcissist's Behavior Get?* YouTube Video.

Dr. Carter, Les. *What Narcissists Misunderstand about Love*. YouTube Video.

Dr. Carter, Les & Cole, T. *Surviving Narcissism*. YouTube Video.

Dr. Ramani. 2021, November 26. *When Malignant Narcissists Love bomb*. YouTube.

Dr. Ramani. 2020, December 10. *The Undetected Way Vulnerable Narcissists Love bomb*. YouTube.

Fisher, H.E. 2004. *Why We Love: the nature & chemistry of romantic love*. New York: H. Holt.

Golden, B. 2022, September 11. *Why the silent treatment is such a destructive form of passive-aggression*. Psychology Today. https://www.psychologytoday.com/us/blog/overcoming-destructive-anger.

Gupta, Sanjay. 2002 *The Chemistry of Love*. Vol 159 (7) p.78. New York: Time Magazine.

Gupta, S. 2022, August 15. *What is the narcissistic abuse cycle?* www.verywellmind.com

Harvard Health. 2007. *Drug Addition and the brain: Effects of dopamine on addiction*. Harvard Health.

Holland, M. 2022, June 8. *Dysfunctional family: Signs, Causes, and the how to Cope*. Choosing Therapy. https://www.choosingtherapy.com

Hotchkiss, S. 2003. *Why Is It Always About You? The Seven Deadly Sins of Narcissism*. New York: Free Press.

Kreger, R. 2012. *Why They Can't Feel Joy: Narcissistic shallow emotions*. https://www.psychologytoday.com

Nadelman, L. 2004. *Research Manual I Childhood Development*. N.J. Lawrence Erlbaum Associates.

Perry, B.D. 2000. *Traumatized children: How childhood trauma influences brain development*. The Journal of the California Alliance for the Mentally Ill.

Reece, G. 2013. *The Trauma Bond/Abusive Relationships*. http://garyreece.blogspot.com.

Resnick, A. 2022, November 23. *What is trauma bonding?* Verywell Mind. https://www.verywellmind.com/trauma- bonding.

Reynolds, C.R. & Kamphaus R.W. editors. 2003. *Handbook of Psychological & Educational Assessment of Children*. New York: Guilford Press.

Salzberg, S. 2020, *Real Change Mindfulness to Heal Ourselves*. New York: Flatiron Books.

Siegel, D.J. 2001. *The Developing Mind: How Relationships and the Brain Interact to Shape Who We Are*. New York: Guilford Press.

Siegel, D.J. & Hartzell, M. 2004. *Parenting from the Inside Out*. New York: Jeremy P. Tarcher.

Smith, Stacy, C; Hung, L. 2021. *Malignant Narcissism: Recognizing a Dangerous Disorder.* New York: Bloomsbury Publications.

Smithstein, S. 2010. *Why It's So Hard to "Just Say No".* psychologytoday.com.

Sterelny, K. & Fitness, J. 2003, *From Mating to Mentality – How the mind works.* Psychology Press.

Tedeschi, R. 2020. *Growth After Trauma.* Harvard Business Review.

Toates, F. 2014. *How Sexual Desire Works.* Cambridge, UK: Cambridge University Press

Twenge, J. M. and Campbell, W. K. 2010. *The Narcissism Epidemic: Living in the Age of Entitlement.* New York: Free Print.

Walker, P. 2013. *Complex PTSD: From surviving to thriving: A guide and map for recovering from childhood trauma.* Azure Coyote Publishing.

Watson, R. 2014. *Oxytocin: The Love and Trust Hormone Can Be Deceptive.* http://psychologytoday.com

WebMD Editors. 2023, March 30. *Narcissism: Symptoms and Signs.* http://www.webmd.com/mental-health/narcissism-symptoms-signs

WebMD Editors. 2022. November 19. *Men and Anger Management. https://www.webme.com/men/guide/anger-management*

ABOUT THE AUTHOR

Vicki Mills holds a B.Ed. from University of Miami an MS and M.Ed. from Florida International University. She answers questions on approximately 40 different FB groups about dealing with narcissistic abusive relationships. Vicki has spent her professional life as an educator, curriculum designer and developer, biologist and fighting for women's rights. She taught Science and Biology, wrote sex education curriculum for Miami Dade County Schools, had a 21-year career with USDA, lived in Hawaii, the Philippines, Hungary, traveled to 65 countries and taught English in China. She enjoys raising her mostly non-narcissistic Burmese cat, painting, growing exotic tropical plants and photography. Her award winning, "Incredible Inside-Out Body" T-Shirt and Owner's Manual, was featured at the "International Year of the Child" Exhibition at the Smithsonian Museum, in two separate exhibitions at their Renwick Gallery in Washington, D.C. She developed a successful course for FIU; "We Are People", to raise awareness of disparate treatment of women and girls. In 2018 at the Tribeca Film Festival, NYC, she was proud to be a part of the cast, interviewed in the acclaimed Netflix documentary, "The Bleeding Edge". An "eye opening look at the medical device industry which reveals how their rush to innovate leads to devastating consequences for patients", (particularly women). With this book, she is sharing a lifetime of hard-won lessons from the caldron of surviving narcissistic abusive relationships. This book has been a labor of love to give women the "know-how" to get through with dignity, self-esteem intact, survive, thrive and move into the emotionally healthy life they deserve.

Made in the USA
Middletown, DE
06 September 2024

59881121R00109